MI at 25

MI at 25

ASSESSING THE IMPACT AND FUTURE
OF MULTIPLE INTELLIGENCES FOR
TEACHING AND LEARNING

Edited by Branton Shearer

TEACHERS
COLLEGE
PRESS

Teachers College, Columbia University
New York and London

Published by Teachers College Press, 1234 Amsterdam Avenue, New York, NY 10027

Library of Congress Cataloging-in-Publication Data

Shearer, Branton.
    MI at 25: assessing the impact and future of multiple intelligences for teaching and learning / edited by Branton Shearer.
        p.   cm.
    Includes bibliographical references and index.
    ISBN 978-0-8077-4999-9 (pbk : alk. paper) — ISBN 978-0-8077-5000-1 (cloth : alk. paper)
    1. Multiple intelligences.   2. Concept learning.   3. Cognitive learning.
4. Education—Curricula.

LB 1062 .M497 2009
370.15'29—dc22

                                                                        2009016350

ISBN: 978-0-8077-4999-9 (paper)
ISBN: 978-0-8077-5000-1 (cloth)

Printed on acid-free paper
Manufactured in the United States of America

16   15   14   13   12   11   10   09   8   7   6   5   4   3   2   1

Contents

MI at 25

Introduction

Branton Shearer

Just a fad or a scientific verity that will stand the test of time?

An idea can be a powerful force. It can send soldiers off to war or spark a scientific revolution that propels people to Mars and beyond. Ideas in education can be notoriously ephemeral and fickle. Many educators have grown wary and skeptical of the latest fad that promises to "revolutionize the classroom." So it caught the educational community off guard that teachers around the world responded with enthusiasm in 1983 when Howard Gardner introduced the theory of multiple intelligences in his seminal book *Frames of Mind: The Theory of Multiple Intelligences*. Multiple intelligences (MI) quickly became one of the most recognized (and perhaps maligned and misunderstood) psychological theories since the invention of the IQ test in the early 1900s.

The impact and validity of MI theory, however, are a matter of great debate even after 25 years. The essays in this collection address several vital issues in the acceptance and implementation of the MI idea that has influenced educators worldwide: Are there convincing arguments and evidence supporting the validity of the eight intelligences? Is MI truly a "scientific theory" that will survive the test of time? What is the impact and contribution of MI theory to classroom practice and school design/reform? What are the cultural barriers and implications for MI-inspired educational practices and research initiatives? Does an MI perspective make positive contributions to an individual's education, self-worth, career development, and community integration? How does MI comport with the long-established notion of *g*, unitary intelligence, as embodied in an IQ score, which forms the foundation of the modern educational edifice (not to mention is enshrined in popular culture)?

A wide variety of perspectives are represented in this book, from the distinctly personal to the multicultural to the highly theoretical to those of recent discoveries in neuroscience. Each author is a respected voice in his or her field, and these essays present ideas, evidence, opinions, and arguments that emerge from many years of in-depth and careful thinking about education, science, art, teaching, psychology, and learning—not to mention that distinctly human metacapacity for theorizing about our theories.

MI theory has broad ramifications, from the very personal to the global, from understanding the vast complexity of neurological events as the brain processes a thought to the invisible cultural mores and assumptions that define who's "smart" and who's not. Ellen Winner and Mihaly Csikszentmihalyi speak directly to the subjective sense of how various conceptions of intelligence affect our well-being, actions, and place in the world. Linda Darling-Hammond describes how a teacher's practice can dramatically alter a student's motivation and engagement in classroom tasks. Deborah Meier describes how an entire school can be formed around a philosophy that respects, honors, and responds to the unique intellectual characteristics of each individual student.

Charles Murray and James R. Flynn provide a challenging view of how social-cultural value systems erect barriers to the acceptance of a "revolutionary" idea that cuts against the grain despite much scientific and theoretical support for its validity. Flynn emphasizes that no culture puts the eight intelligences on an equal footing. Each culture has a language that reflects its own peculiar hierarchy. Does anyone think we could flatten the hierarchy by relabeling? So how much contribution will the relabeling of intelligence make in American education? Noam Chomsky has probed the depths of human language structures and in the process was a leader in the "cognitive revolution" that undermined the dominance of radical behaviorism. He finds notable similarities between his work on linguistic structures/human cognition and the multiple intelligences. Chomsky observes that while MI is a worthy "hypothesis" about human intelligence, it doesn't yet meet the standards of a fully developed "scientific theory." Marc Hauser picks up on this theme and describes how he refuses to even use the word *intelligence* as he pursues his pathbreaking research into human and animal cognition. Michael Posner reports that there are large numbers of neuroscientific studies that are generally supportive of the MI framework. But there remains a great deal of work to do to fully test the adequacy of the MI model as an accurate and useful description of the brain's intellectual structures and functions.

Each contributor was asked to reflect on the impact, status, and future viability of MI theory from the perspective of his or her discipline. It is obvious that despite great cultural barriers, MI theory's impact has been felt broadly and deeply. It emerged at a time that was both fortuitous as well as unfortunate. The idea that intelligence is more than a single ability has been pretty much buried in both the psychological and educational literatures. The debate now is really which model of *multiple* intelligences will be accepted. Which model best describes the functions of the brain and yet also serves the needs of students and the institutions of global education? Does intelligence have three parts, eight dimensions, 120 domains, or more? Can feelings and emotions be reasonably classified as intellectual skills? Is intelligence something more than logical problem solving?

MI arrived at the classroom door of millions of teachers at just the right time. By 1983 it was patently obvious to entire schools (and in some countries, their whole educational system) that a single number was an entirely inadequate way to describe the abilities of their students. For years teachers have been grappling with various notions of *learning styles* to help them understand the perplexing differences in students' thinking. But conceptions of learning styles are fuzzy and lack the gravitas of intelligence and so IQ remains the cornerstone of a school's curriculum. This, of course, matches with the priorities of the age of information and technology—math, science, and reading reign supreme as the hallmarks of an *intelligent* person.

For more than 25 years public schools have been under siege by politicians for "underperforming" and "failing students"; this drumbeat reached a crescendo, coincidently in 1983, with the publication of *A Nation in Crisis* and the clarion call provoked by the "rising tide of mediocrity": Something must be done! thundered America's leaders. They responded to a 20th-century problem with a 19th-century, industrial, "top down" solution—We must standardize the curriculum! Demand higher test scores (productivity)! Get our money's worth from our educational investment dollars! Increase quality control! Maximize efficiency! These solutions are all based on the assumption that we can measure *all* the intellectual products of *all* students in a standardized and cost-efficient manner, assuming that test and IQ scores are valid representations of the best that the human mind is capable of. MI theory poses a direct and devastating challenge to that basic assumption.

Or does it? Charles Murray poses a cease-fire in the intelligence wars with his suggestion that all parties agree to stop fighting over the word *intelligence* and simply use *abilities* in its stead. A noble proposal, but it assumes that willing psychologists can wrestle the former term out of the

grip of popular consciousness and that the IQ-testing and -research establishment will give up its proprietary claims to the concept so easily. Would
the Wechsler Adult Intelligence Scale willingly change its name (and fundamental assumptions) to Adult Abilities Scale? Would school psychologists
accept this change and modify their terminology? It also assumes that
governmental regulators will not evaluate school effectiveness based primarily on reading and math test scores. Not likely. I wonder . . . would it
be better to incorporate IQ, intellectual styles, and emotional sensitivity
within an integrated model of multiple intelligences? In such a model MI
would be understood as a natural evolution rather than a revolution in our
understanding of the intellectual capacities of the brain. See Chapter 1 for
more details.

As we learn about the complexity and structures of the brain (and
cultures) we can continue to design a mosaic model of human intelligences
that recognizes the true value of the full range of thinking skills. With a
coherent and nuanced model of intelligence that accords with emerging
neuroscience, we can then honor the strengths of traditional educational
structures and evolve innovative curricula that serve the more "real world"
abilities displayed by large numbers of students from a wide diversity of
backgrounds. This would not entail a watering down of the concept of
intelligence and standards of high-quality work, but instead would add a
full-color, high-definition view to our black-and-white IQ test results.

Of course, we want math wizards to design and operate the next generation of supercomputers. Naturally, we need articulate writers of technical manuals and meaningful stories. But we also want the visually keen
graphic designer to create a pleasing interface for the everyday computer
user. We will all benefit from the interpersonally astute software creator
who makes games that promote peaceful conflict resolutions among friends
and neighbors (perhaps nations?). The intrapersonally intelligent televi-
sion producer may guide us all on how best to use cutting-edge media for
stress and anxiety reduction, career planning, and lifelong learning strategies. The musicians, actors, and dancers who consult with our nations'
lawmakers may guide the next generation of leaders on how to enhance
creative thinking in the council chambers, board rooms, executive offices,
and departments of energy as we wrestle with economic, environmental,
and cultural challenges to our health and well-being.

It can be daunting to reconsider all the personal and cultural assumptions that have been invested in our concept of human intelligence—let
alone animal intelligence! But such a reconsideration can have profound
consequences for the practical tasks of instructing, advising, and curriculum building and for our daily interactions with significant others. Do we
peg them at a particular level (smart, merely average, or dull) on a single
ladder of "smartness"? Do we value a new colleague's emotional sensitiv-

ity as an important on-the-job ability? Or do we denigrate a child's creative thinking on the playground knowing how poorly he or she performs on math tests?

Perhaps 25 years is too short a time period to adequately judge the fate of any unique and peculiar idea such as MI, but it's not too soon to propose how it can serve as a bridge from where we've been to where we know that we *must* go—if we are not merely to survive, but rather, to thrive as a unique and peculiar species on this particular and spectacular planet!

It has been said, "What people are most afraid of is what they don't understand. When they don't understand something they rely on their assumptions, which often turn out to be quite wrong, but they'll defend them with a vehemence that defies logic and inhibits learning." It is my hope that these essays and interviews will shed more light than heat in our quest to describe the mystery of human intelligence that shines forth in even the mundane tasks of our everyday lives. From this knowledge will come creative strategies to teach, counsel, and guide people to maximize their intellectual potential.

Intelligence: In Theory, in Daily Life, and in the Brain

Branton Shearer

Philosophers, psychologists, scientists, educators, and people in daily life have used a wide variety of definitions for *intelligence* since time immemorial. For the ancient Greeks the essence of intelligence was "rationality" and logical reasoning. In ancient China an educated person was one who was skilled in various arts, including calligraphy, singing, and rhetoric. To grasp the current status and possible future of multiple intelligences theory, it is helpful to have an understanding of its relationship to modern conceptions of intelligence and something of their social/cultural/historical contexts.

In *Frames of Mind: The Theory of Multiple Intelligences* Gardner (1993) provided extensive research to support his contention that human intelligence is best conceptualized as seven relatively independent faculties (the eighth, naturalist, was added in 1996). Gardner redefined *intelligence* as "a biopsychological potential to process information that can be activated in a cultural setting to solve problems or create products that are of value in a culture" (1999, p. 34). Gardner's definition of intelligence is unique because it includes divergent as well as convergent thinking abilities and also connects the thinking skills within the individual with what is valued by his or her culture.

To qualify as an intelligence in Gardner's scheme, each ability has to satisfy a range of criteria: the potential for isolated breakdown of the skill through brain damage; the existence of savants, prodigies, and other exceptional individuals with this ability; support from psychological training studies and from psychometric studies, including correlations across tests; evolutionary plausibility; and a distinct developmental history culminating in a definable set of end state performances. In addition, each intelligence has to have an identifiable core operation or set of operations, as well as susceptibility to coding in a symbol system (such as language, mathematics, picturing, or musical notes) (Feldman, 1998). See Chapter 7 for more details.

Eight distinct intelligences to date sufficiently meet these criteria to be included on the list, including linguistic, logical-mathematical, spatial, kinesthetic, musical, naturalist, interpersonal, and intrapersonal. The intelligences are broad categories of ability composed of specific sets of skills evident in daily life; for example, musical intelligence includes instrumental skill, vocal talent, and so on. These skills are used either individually or in combination for various culturally defined expressions, such as jazz, folk, classical, or easy listening music.

A SKETCH OF THE HISTORY OF INTELLIGENCE

The following briefly describes several of the major theories of intelligence that have been most influential in the Western world for the past few hundred years. It is not meant to be a definitive history, but rather it illustrates how the concept of intelligence has been altered over time and the relationship of these changes to MI theory. It is important to note that (despite some arguments to the contrary) the word *intelligence* is an abstract term that every person and every culture defines differently according to his or her or to its own time and place. It is rather like the concept of beauty, always changing according to the fashions of the day.

Of course, how such terms are defined at any particular time and place can have profound implications for the fate of individuals. A woman who would have been considered beautiful and treated as royalty in the Middle Ages would be ignored and probably denigrated by today's pencil-thin fashion industry standards. Likewise, a boy regarded as intelligent for hunting and hand-to-hand combat may today be out of step with the needs of the 21st-century "knowledge economy." The point is that definitions are important and can have significant and lasting impact on the lives of specific individuals as well as institutions that are charged with educating young people and developing human potential. This is of particular importance now and will be in the future as our scientific understanding of the structures and systems of the brain are interpreted by individual scientists within particular cultures. Understanding the workings of those 100 billion neurons and their immeasurable synaptic interconnections depends upon the clarity and authenticity of our "definitions" and "concepts."

In the late 1800s in England, Francis Galton (1883) measured intelligence with tests of physical abilities, measuring reaction time, hearing sensitivity, endurance, weight discrimination, pain endurance, visual acuteness, and olfactory sensitivity. These tests were viewed by many as representing significant progress, superior to the very popular "science" of phrenology wherein a person's intelligence, along with many personality characteristics, were described by reading the pattern of bumps on the person's head.

Another advance in the understanding of intelligence came in 1904 in France when Alfred Binet devised the first empirically based test of cognitive abilities. However, Binet refused to claim that his test actually measured intelligence because he believed that intelligence was too complicated to be measured by a single test. He was quoted by L. M. Terman in 1921: "This scale [Binet's 1905 series of tests], properly speaking, does not permit the *measurement* [italics added] of intelligence, because intellectual properties . . . can not be measured as linear surfaces are measured, but are, on the contrary, a classification, a hierarchy among diverse intelligences" (p. 130).

Binet described intelligence in practical terms such as judgment, good sense, initiative and the ability to adapt one's self to changing circumstances (Binet & Simon, 1916). His test was found to be a good predictor for children who would do well in school and those who would be in need of special assistance. Within a few years, Binet's test was adapted for widespread use in Great Britain and the United States and became the basis for psychoeducational testing worldwide. Even today it continues to serve as a basic yardstick against which almost all tests of IQ are measured.

The notion of a unitary intelligence, or what became known as g (for "general intelligence"), was greatly advanced with the development of sophisticated statistical procedures that allowed psychologists to give IQ-based tests to large numbers of people and then analyze the resulting pattern of correlations in test scores. A sophisticated statistical procedure called *factor analysis* was used by Charles Spearman (1927) and others to empirically "prove" that g underlies all important cognitive activity. They found a moderate correlation in test scores in a battery of verbal and quantitative tests. These tests coincide with the skills required for successful participation in traditional academic programs. They also happen to be strongly associated with socioeconomic status and parents' level of education.

Surprisingly, IQ theory is really a "multiple" intelligence model, because along with a "general ability" are described a number of vaguely defined "specific abilities" (physical, vision, and so on) that are ignored (denigrated) in the literature because they are not associated with academic accomplishment. Instead, the rise of "scientific psychology" has required that there be a single, quantifiable measure of intelligence in the form of a mental *object* that could be subjected to various statistical manipulations.

So for all intents and purposes IQ theory is a "unitary" theory of intelligence in both academic and popular contexts.

Other statistically oriented psychologists have interpreted test data differently and come to an opposite conclusion that intelligence is, indeed, multifaceted rather than unitary. In 1938 Louis Thurstone produced research data that argues for at least seven primary mental abilities: verbal comprehension; verbal fluency; inductive reasoning; spatial visualization; and number, memory, and perceptual speed.

By the 1950s, J. P. Guilford (1954) introduced scientific evidence that intelligence is composed of somewhere between 120 and 150 "factors of mind." Guilford defined intelligence according to three dimensions: operations, contents, and products. This model has had great appeal for its scope and comprehensiveness by including both academic skills as well as creative thinking. But it has been found to be too complex and unwieldy to be adopted for serious use and thus has fallen into disfavor.

However, also during the 1950s the pioneering "split brain" neuropsychological research of Roger Sperry (1961) sparked the widespread acceptance of "learning styles." The concept of learning or cognitive style is difficult to define because there are such a wide variety of models. Many theories describe a person's learning *likes/dislikes* or thinking *preferences* or dominant sensory *modalities* (Bandler & Grinder, 1979; Dunn & Dunn, 1993; Dunn, Dunn, & Price, 1984; Keirsy & Bates, 1984; Kolb, 1985; Silver, Strong, & Perini, 2000; Sternberg, 1997). Some theories emphasize a person's interests, while others describe personality characteristics, and still others focus on environmental conditions. An important distinction must be made, however, between intelligence and style. A person's *abilities* or *skills* are part of his or her intelligence and are not the same as *interests* or *preferences*. They may be correlated or they may not. Gardner reminds us that it is a conceptual error to conflate these two ideas.

One learning style theory familiar to most teachers is the V, A, K model (Dunn, Dunn, & Price, 1984), which states that a child may prefer to learn something through visual, auditory, or kinesthetic sensory modalities. This is also known as the "see it, hear it, and do it" approach. There are obvious connections between the V, A, K model with the Visual, Linguistic, and Kinesthetic intelligences, but unfortunately it is all too easy to confuse *interest* with *ability*. A student may have a keen interest in athletics but very little actual skill in coordination, dexterity, or balance. Another student may have perfect musical pitch but detest singing and never listen to music or play an instrument.

Teachers use learning style language to help them understand students who they know are not "stupid" but who may struggle with academic skills and receive low IQ-related test scores. It is still common to hear people who are creative/artistic as being "right brained" and those who are good at math as being "left brained." These concepts evolved from the early "split brain" studies that found that the right and left hemispheres of a typical human brain process information differently (Sperry, 1961). Much more recent neuroscience evidence informs us that these dichotomous descriptions grossly oversimplify the complexity of the brain's functions. Various personality theorists have elaborated on these distinctions in learning *style* with descriptions such as introverted, reflective, action oriented, intuitive, conforming, mastery oriented, and concrete versus abstract thinking (Jung, 1969; Kolb, 1985; and many others). These descriptions emphasize enduring personality traits, temperaments, habits, and preferences rather than competencies.

The unitary model of intelligence embodied by an IQ score has been validated against and correlates with tests of logical reasoning, verbal facility, vocabulary, numerical reasoning, abstract thinking, attention, and rapid processing of information (Wechsler, 1958). In learning style vernacular, almost all these tests can be described as being "left brained" dominant activities that neglect more artistic and intuitive thinking. An influential theory of intelligence that strives to correct this bias and that uses standard IQ tests is the two-factor cognitive model: fluid and crystallized (Cattell, 1971; Horn, 1967).

Fluid intelligence gives one the ability to understand abstract and often novel relations. Crystallized intelligence is composed of one's accumulation of knowledge and general information. These correspond approximately with the performance and verbal sections of standardized IQ test batteries. They are also embedded within each of the multiple intelligences. A carpenter must use spatial memories to accurately follow a blueprint but then innovate when confronted with novel situations. This model is embedded in a number of learning style theories.

While learning style language may be useful to teachers, it leaves intact the core assumption that only IQ-related abilities represent a person's "true intelligence." A student may be merely "artistic" and still not considered to have real "intelligence." MI theory challenges the fundamental assumption that one form of intelligence (such as logical-mathematical) is of greater value than any of the others. Learning style theories may describe a person's preferences for processing information but they do not account for the actual value of the resulting products or problems that are solved.

Many concepts in the "information processing" model of intelligence are informed by Jean Piaget's theories of cognitive development in which intellectual abilities evolve through several fairly discrete and yet qualitatively different stages of development (Piaget, 1950). These stages are loosely associated with developmental age: (1) sensorimotor, (2) intuitive (preoperational), (3) concrete operations, (4) formal operations, and (5) post-formal operations (as posited by neo-Piagetian theorists).

A critique of the Piaget model does not argue that it isn't an accurate description of the evolution of the logical thinking skills, but instead suggests that it is a bare and somewhat misleading framework. Viewed from the multiple intelligences perspective it is easy to see that at each stage there are more intelligences involved in these "cognitive tasks" than merely logical thinking. A few obvious examples are the following:

Sensorimotor = kinesthetic + logical
Intuitive = visual-spatial + logical
Concrete operations = spatial + logical (kinesthetic?)
Formal operations = logical + intrapersonal + interpersonal.

But these examples are incomplete also because they only describe shifts in emphasis at each stage when in fact the "whole child's mind" is evolving so that many different intelligences may or may not be developing at the same pace and in the same way.

The intuitive child's capacity for creating imaginative worlds can be expressed visually (finger painting), verbally (fantastic stories), and kinesthetically in dramatic gestures that are associated with new interpersonal understanding (role playing) and heightened self-talk (intrapersonal and linguistic). Another shift in emphasis is that the Piagetian model for the developing child is one in which the child is primarily a "scientist." The MI definition of intelligence equally values the growing child as "artist" and "humanist" as well as "scientist."

MI theory poses this challenge to the Piagetian model: "What happens to each of the other intelligences as the child progresses through each stage?" For some reason they are not described in the Piagetian model. I don't think they disappear from the child's mind/brain repertoire unless large portions of the brain should happen to be removed or disabled. No, what happens in this model is that they are ignored because their value to the logical thinking process is not considered to be of importance (*merely* "specific abilities," "aptitudes," or "talents") in this implicitly Western European view. In fact, it is commonly assumed that the other intelligences (especially those closely associated with physical abilities and emotion) are undesirable and detrimental to logical thinking.

A similar split has occurred throughout the history of cognitive science when the attentional, memory, and problem-solving processes were defined as abstract unitary domains and studied apart from their physical embodiments and their emotional attributes. This was probably necessary because of the historical limitations in scientific technology and models that encouraged reducing the variables under study to their bare minimum. This is a useful approach, but deceptive in its simplicity. The corollary in physical science is the evolution from Newtonian mechanistic theories to the dialectical and relativistic models dominant in the post-Einstein age.

Neuroscience evidence continues to support the MI model that each intelligence possesses its own relatively distinct memory system (verbal, visual, kinesthetic, self, and so on) (see below). Problem-solving skills are likewise contextual and "intelligence dependent." The same in all probability holds true for attention and concentration in daily life (Posner & Rothbart, 2007).

A third assumption of cognitive intelligence is that its essential core is the ability of rapid reasoning. Thus, timed tests or logical problem solving is the essential feature of nearly all intelligence tests. MI theory recognizes this ability as a valued skill, but equally values metacognitive, reflective thinking that may not be fast and may also not appear to be "logical." Instead, knowledge and understanding may be obtained through self-reflection, insight, and empathy. What this means is that we cannot fully test or assess each intelligence without taking into account these more "performance" and context-dependent skills.

Psychologists who are most critical of MI are those who point to the cultural value of g as a scientific verity that accounts for academic achievement. They argue (wrongly) that MI denies the existence of this statistically proved "fact." Indeed, g may well be a moderately positive predictor of school success, but MI broadens the question (to the chagrin of its critics) to ask: What combinations of intelligences (beyond the logical-mathematical and linguistic that compose g) might account for success in real world endeavors beyond the classroom? Perhaps the kinesthetic and interpersonal intelligences combine to form a performer g? The master technician may depend upon a spatial and logical skill combination. The humanist and the novelist may exploit differing aspects of the interpersonal, linguistic and intrapersonal intelligences. Important questions like these are addressed by MI theory in very specific and practical ways to enhance personal growth, career development, and educational planning (see accompanying chart).

The theory of emotional intelligence articulated by Salovey and Mayer (1990) and later popularized by Daniel Goleman (1995) provided another answer to the question, "What does it mean to be intelligent?" Goleman argues that academic intelligence is important to success, but that emotional competency is even more important. He defines emotional intelligence as comprising such abilities as managing relationships, motivating oneself, persistence, impulse control, empathy, and mood regulation.

Emotional intelligence is the ability to recognize and manage feelings and moods in oneself and in other people. Emotional intelligence is based in part on neuroscience evidence as well as the interpersonal and intrapersonal aspects of the multiple intelligences. However, Gardner argues that emotional intelligence is better described as "emotional sensitivity" because it forms only part of the more comprehensive entities of the intrapersonal and interpersonal intelligences. He further argues that it is a conceptual error to define prosocial behavior as more "emotionally intelligent" because in MI theory all the intelligences are amoral "tools" and thus can be used for good or ill. For example, any effective leader (Gandhi, the head of a street gang, Lincoln, a mob boss, Mao, Lenin, Tito) can use his or her keen emotional sensitivity and insights to lead people either into genocidal war or to freedom.

MI theory does not have to be viewed as a stand-alone model but rather works well when merged with Bloom's taxonomy (1956). This framework is frequently used by educators to describe the quality of thought involved in school-based learning activities. The revised Bloom taxonomy of educational objectives (Anderson & Krathwohl, 2001) charts a hierarchy of six stages of thought from the most basic level of engagement—*Remember*—to the highest level—*Create*. The intermediate levels are *Understand*, *Apply*, *Analyze*, and *Evaluate*. These categories of thinking/performance are easily mapped onto activities pertaining to each of the multiple intelligences to create a dynamic assessment matrix. Noble (2004) provides a practical framework that integrates the Bloom/MI matrix to assist teachers in providing differentiated instruction. For example, the basic level of kinesthetic intelligence would be to remember the steps of a dance. At the highest levels, choreographers create new forms of dance and are able to critique and evaluate the strengths and limitations of movement phrases, expressions, and gestures.

A widely influential model of multiple intelligences described by Robert Sternberg (1985) is the Triarchic model, which posits that there are three different kinds of intellectual abilities: analytical (academic), practical, and creative. Sternberg is somewhat vague in his definition of intelligence, but most recently has defined "successful intelligence" as that which allows people to "achieve important goals" through a combination of his three intelligence forms. Sternberg's view of intelligence appears to have evolved toward a unitary, generic theory in which the three strands are woven into a single thread in a person's life.

Sternberg (Sternberg et al., 1996) describes creatively intelligent people as being able to discover, create, and invent, especially in the realm of creating ideas that are both novel and valuable. Practical intelligence involves "using, utilizing, and applying knowledge." Practical thinking can involve everyday verbal reasoning, everyday math, and figural thinking involving map reading and navigation. People who are strong in the analytical/academic intelligence are good at logical analysis, evaluation, and critique. Analytical skill is noted to be critical to success in academic subjects, but according to Sternberg it is also used outside school

Multiple Intelligences Definitions and Sample Corresponding Careers

MI	Core Skills	Domains	Careers
Musical	To think in sounds, rhythms, melodies, and rhymes. To be sensitive to pitch, rhythm, timbre, and tone. To recognize, create, and reproduce music by using an instrument or voice. To engage in active listening and identify connections between music and emotions.	Vocal Instrumental Appreciation Rhythm	Choir director Music teacher Songwriter Vocalist
Kinesthetic	To think in movements and to use the body in skilled and complicated ways for expressive and goal directed activities. A sense of timing, coordination for whole body movement, and the use of hands for manipulating objects.	Athletics Dance Expressive movement Fine-motor control	Athlete Choreographer Dancer Actor
Logical-Mathematical	To think of cause and effect connections and to understand relationships between actions, objects, or ideas. To calculate, quantify, or consider propositions and perform complex mathematical or logical operations. Involves inductive and deductive reasoning skills and creative problem solving.	Calculations Logical reasoning Problem solving Analysis	Accountant Computer repair person Electrical engineer Scientist
Spatial	To think in pictures and to understand the visual/spatial world. To think in three dimensions and to transform one's perceptions and re-create aspects of one's visual experience via imagination. To work with objects effectively.	Mental imagery/ visualization Spatial orientation Artistic design Working with objects	Architect Pilot Interior designer Artist

(continued)

Multiple Intelligences (*continued*)

MI	Core Skills	Domains	Careers
Linguistic	To think in words and to use language to express and understand complex meanings. Sensitivity to the meaning of words and the order among words, sounds, rhythms, and inflections. To reflect on the use of language in everyday life.	Reading Writing Speaking Listening comprehension	Attorney Journalist Poet Public relations director
Interpersonal	To think about and understand another person. To have empathy and recognize distinctions among people and to appreciate their perspectives with sensitivity to their motives, moods and intentions. Involves interacting effectively with one or more people in familiar, casual, or working circumstances.	Empathy Interpersonal perspective taking Managing relationships Group management	Counselor Nurse Salesperson Teacher
Intrapersonal	To think about and understand one's self. To be aware of one's strengths and weaknesses and to plan effectively to achieve personal goals. Reflecting on and monitoring one's thoughts and feelings and regulating them effectively. The ability to monitor oneself in inter-personal relationships and to act with personal efficacy.	Metacognition Affective management Personal life management Decision-making and judgment	CEO Clergy member Entrepreneur Psychologist
Naturalist	To understand the natural world, including plants, animals, and scientific studies. To recognize, name, and classify individuals, species, and ecological relationships. To interact effectively with living creatures and discern patterns of life and natural forces.	Understanding animals Understanding plants Pattern recognition Understanding natural forces	Biologist Farmer Meteorologist Veterinarian

for problem solving, decision making, and mathematical reasoning. Sternberg believes that analytical ability is measured somewhat effectively by IQ-type tests, but not fully because such tests do not cover analytical thinking in daily life.

An integrated model of multiple intelligences can readily be constructed by interweaving each of Gardner's eight intelligences with Sternberg's three cognitive styles (Shearer, 2006). Such a model addresses two questions about MI: What are the particular manifestations of an individual's intellectual propensities? and How can MI theory's broad general categories be investigated by the tools of neuroscience that associate neural events with very specific activities? For example, musical intelligence can be expressed creatively through cultural domains instrumentally (jazz piano, guitar riffs) or vocally (opera, scat singing) or rhythmically (drum solos). Visual-spatial intelligence can be expressed practically (plumbing, carpentry, road construction) and creatively (abstract painting, sculpture, fashion) and analytically (statistical graphs, textbook illustrations).

IQ test scores (in the form of their many surrogates) serve in modern schools as gatekeepers and tracking devices. A certain score must be attained to be considered for inclusion in gifted and special education programs/services. Groups of students are assigned to particular educational tracks: slow, average, and accelerated, based on scores. Aggregate reading and math test scores are used to judge the quality of a school's effectiveness. The MI-inspired educational philosophy advocates not for "grouping" but rather for the "personalization" of instruction and curriculum based upon the recognition of each individual student's strengths and limitations. Simplistic, superficial, and stereotypical interpretation of a student's MI profile is strongly discouraged.

THE EIGHT MULTIPLE INTELLIGENCES
AND THEIR PARTICULAR EXPRESSIONS

The eight intelligences each has its own memory system with cerebral structures involved with processing its specific contents. As our scientific knowledge increases it is possible that the list of intelligences will change accordingly. In fact, at the time of this writing Gardner is reviewing the scientific evidence regarding a possible ninth intelligence, existential. The core components of the eight intelligences are briefly summarized below along with their associated Triarchic styles.

Career implications are also briefly listed. Gardner has written that skillful performance in most real-world tasks requires the smooth integration of several intelligences working in concert. A successful career usually requires strengths in two or perhaps three intelligences and tertiary skills. For example, a lawyer needs to be strong logically and linguistically, but the trial lawyer will also use interpersonal skills to leverage success. A contracts lawyer uses the strength of logic in the written word to solve complex problems.

Linguistic and logical-mathematical intelligences are most often associated with academic accomplishment and are the primary elements of general intelligence (*g*). The core features of linguistic intelligence include the ability to use words effectively for reading, writing, listening, and speaking. Linguistic skill is important for providing explanations, descriptions, and expressiveness. Gardner describes the poet as the epitome of linguistic ability. Other career fields requiring skill in this area include teaching, journalism, and psychology. Convergent aspects of linguistic intelligence assessed by standard intelligence tests include vocabulary and reading comprehension. Activities requiring divergent thinking include story telling, persuasive speech, and creative writing.

Logical-mathematical intelligence involves skill in calculations as well as logical reasoning and problem solving. People strong in this intelligence are usually the ones who are described as being "smart" (mathematicians, philosophers, logicians, engineers). Logical-mathematical intelligence is required for multistep, complex problem solving and mental math. Most IQ tests assess a person's ability to reason logically and problem-solve quickly, but do not examine divergent and reflective aspects of logical-mathematical intelligence. Divergent aspects of this intelligence include curiosity, the identification of novel problems, and the generation of new and worthy questions.

Musical intelligence includes sensitivity to pitch, rhythm, timbre, and the emotional aspects of sound as pertaining to the functional areas of musical appreciation, singing, and playing an instrument. A composer requires significant skill in many aspects of this intelligence—especially involving creative musical thinking. On the other hand, some musical careers (instrumentalist, vocalist) may require more circumscribed abilities that emphasize technical skill rather than creative output.

Kinesthetic intelligence highlights the ability to use one's body in highly skilled ways for both expressive (dance, acting) and goal-directed activities (athletics, working with one's hands). Well-developed kinesthetic ability for innovative movement is required for success in professions such as choreography, acting, and directing movies or plays. Precision, control, and agility are the hallmarks of athletes such as karate masters, professional soccer players, and gymnasts. Brain surgeons and diamond cutters must have well-developed fine-motor dexterity, while modern dancers and mimes are able to express complex abstract ideas through subtle gestures and movements.

Spatial intelligence includes the ability to understand the physical world and to perform transformations and modifications upon one's perceptions via mental imagery. Functional aspects of spatial intelligence include artistic design, map making/reading, and working with objects. Visual artists and interior designers exemplify creative spatial thinking, and a successful architect will need both creative abilities as well as technical expertise. An automobile mechanic or engineer, on the other hand, may rarely need creative or artistic abilities to find the solution to a malfunctioning engine.

A person strong in the *naturalist* intelligence displays empathy, recognition, and understanding for living and natural things (plants, animals, geology). Those in careers requiring strong naturalist skills include farmers, scientists, naturalists and animal behaviorists. Skilled scientists use pattern recognition to identify an individual's species classification, create taxonomies, and understand ecological systems. Empathic understanding is a related ability that allows people to care for and manage the behavior of living entities.

Unique contributions of the MI model to intelligence theory are the personal intelligences. The *intrapersonal* and *interpersonal* intelligences are presented as separate yet related functions of the human brain (especially the frontal lobes). Intrapersonal ability emphasizes self-knowledge and interpersonal involves understanding other people.

Vital functions of *intrapersonal* intelligence include accurate self-appraisal, goal setting, self-monitoring/correction, and emotional self-management. Results of research have highlighted the importance of metacognition for learning in the basic academic skills of reading and mathematics. Intrapersonal intelligence is not the same as self-esteem, but the former may be a strong factor in promoting self-confidence and effective stress management. Well-developed intrapersonal intelligence may well be essential to an individual's sense of satisfaction and success. Intrapersonal intelligence is the royal road to achievement, learning, and personal satisfaction, and thus is key to maximizing career success. Those in specific vocations that require skills in intrapersonal self-management include pilots, police officers, writers, counselors, and teachers.

Interpersonal intelligence also plays a vital function in a person's sense of well-being. It promotes success in managing relationships with other people. Its two central skills, the ability to notice and make distinctions between other individuals and the ability to recognize the emotions, moods, perspectives, and motivations of people, are known to be critical factors in successful employment. The ability to manage groups of people is required for managerial or leadership positions. Good teachers, counselors, salespeople, and psychologists need to understand a specific individual and then be adept at managing that relationship.

EACH INTELLIGENCE IS ASSOCIATED WITH SPECIFIC NEUROPSYCHOLOGICAL SYSTEMS

In response to the question "Does brain research continue to support your theory?" Howard Gardner responded:

> The accumulating neurological evidence is amazingly supportive of the general thrust of MI theory. Research supports the particular intelligences that I have described and provides elegant evidence of the fine structure of such capacities as linguistic, mathematical, and musical processing. At the same time, this research calls into some question an effort to localize each intelligence at a specific point in the brain. It makes more sense now to speak of several brain areas involved in any complex intellectual activity, and to highlight the extent to which different individuals may carry out a certain function using different portions of their respective brains.
>
> It is sometimes argued that MI theory is questionable because the brain is a very flexible organ subject to the events of early experience. This remark is not pertinent, since "neural plasticity" is independent of the issue of different intelligences. MI theory demands that linguistic processing, for example, occur via a different set of neural mechanisms than does spatial processing. The fact that the processing may occur in somewhat different regions of the brain for different people, because of their early experiences, is interesting but irrelevant to the identification of intelligences per se. (1999, p. 99)

The question also arises of how closely linked the intelligences are to cerebral structures. While there are specific neural structures that are closely and undeniably linked to the core components of each intelligence, it is better to think of the brain as having sets of "cerebral systems" that are primarily responsible for processing the specific contents associated with each intelligence. It is a task for future researchers to describe these links in greater detail and to provide a general neurological framework for better interpreting neuroscientific data and understanding the multiple intelligences.

The first MI-neural networks were sketched by Gardner in 1983 primarily on the basis of cerebral lesions, the only available evidence at the time. Since then numerous sophisticated technologies have provided many insights into the functions of brain systems and structures. Of course, the human brain is one of the world's most complex functioning entities with a near infinite range of interconnections so exact delineations between functional systems are difficult to describe with precision. To make matters even more challenging, structures often serve dual or even multiple purposes, while other structures have limited and dedicated functions.

Musical Neural Systems

Musical intelligence is primarily associated with the neural structures in the right anterior temporal and frontal lobes. The right auditory cortex is involved in perceiving pitch, melody, harmony, timbre, and rhythm (Perez & Gagnon, 1999). Researchers have correlated the cognitive aspects of music processing (musical syntax and meaning) with a complex network involving these structures: inferior frontal gyrus, superior temporal sulcus, and the supramarginal gyrus (Koelsch, Kritz, Schulze, Alsop, & Schlaug, 2005). The right and left planum temporale structures are important for the perception of both music and the sounds of human language (Schlaug, Jancke, & Steinmetz, 1995).

Spatial Neural Systems

Spatial intelligence is primarily associated with right hemisphere, parietal posterior, and occipital lobe systems. Vision is first processed in the occipital lobe, but spatial intelligence involves more than vision. The brains of people born blind can process spatial information in the absence of visual input in the parietal lobe. Cognitive representations of the "outer world" are processed by the so-called grid cells in the entorhinal cortex, hippocampus, and medial temporal lobe (Hafting, 2005).

Kinesthetic Neural Systems

Kinesthetic intelligence is most associated with the cerebral motor strip, thalamus, basal ganglia, and cerebellum. Large-motor movements activate the cerebral motor strip on both the right and left sides of the brain. A major responsibility of the cerebellum and basal ganglia is the smooth coordination of fine motor movements (Gazzaniga, 1999).

Linguistic Neural Systems

Linguistic intelligence is one of the most studied of neural capacities and for most people it involves the left hemisphere's temporal and frontal lobes. Classic neurological studies beginning in the mid 1800s described how damaged areas of the left hemisphere differentially impaired language functions. Neuroscientists have now clarified that the lateral sulcus loop (the fissure of Sylvius) in the left hemisphere of the brain is a neural system that is involved in both understanding and producing spoken language. Broca's area in the left inferior frontal cortex processes the production and syntactic aspects of speech. Carl Wernicke discovered that damage to the lower portion of the left temporal lobe impairs language comprehension and results in speech that is fluid but incoherent.

A more recently discovered third language area, the inferior parietal lobule of the left hemisphere, is crucial for understanding the multiple properties of spoken and written words: their sound, appearance, function, and other features. This particular area may thus help the brain to classify and label things, which is an essential prerequisite for concept formation and abstract thought (Douglas Hospital Research Centre, 2002).

Logical-mathematical Neural Systems

Logical-mathematical intelligence involves a complex network of systems including the left parietal lobes and adjacent temporal and occipital association areas. This system shares some of the structures and functions associated with language (concept formation) as described above, but numerical cognition places a particular emphasis on the intraparietal sulcus. The angular gyrus is also involved in processing numerical magnitude (Cappelletti et al., 2007). Logical thought activates the right hemisphere spatial organization tasks, while the frontal system becomes involved in planning and goal setting.

Naturalist Neural Systems

Naturalist intelligence is one of the least studied of intelligences and less is known about its cerebral bases. There is limited evidence that areas of the left parietal lobe are responsible for discriminating living from nonliving things (Gaffin & Heywood, 1993). There is some speculation that species recognition is processed differently by different people. Some people may rely more on visual information while others may emphasize auditory, tactile, or perhaps olfactory (Gardner, 1999).

Intrapersonal and Interpersonal Neural Systems

The frontal lobes of the brain are known to be crucial integrating stations for knowledge regarding one's self and the understanding of other people. Intrapersonal intelligence involves awareness of one's own thoughts, feelings, and behavior. The prefrontal cortex is connected to the emotional processing amygdala so that we can choose how to respond to a fear-evoking stimulus. Autobiographical memory is associated with several prefrontal areas along with the hippocampus in the construction of a self-history (Cabeza & St. Jacques, 2007). Metacognitive activities, also known as executive functions (planning, goal setting, evaluation, conflict resolution), activate midlevel frontal lobe structures, including the anterior cingulate, the supplementary motor area, the orbitofrontal cortex, the dorsolateral prefrontal cortex, and portions of the basal ganglia and the thalamus (Fernandez-Duque, Baird, & Posner, 2000).

Interpersonal intelligence has been studied extensively as empathy, theory of mind, and social understanding. The neural systems involved in social empathy are shared with self-awareness of feelings. The loop between the frontal lobes and the anterior temporal lobe (amygdala and insular cortex) are thought to be crucial for empathy (Goleman, 1995, 2006). Social deficits were linked by researchers to the ventromedial prefrontal, parietal, and cingulated areas as well as the right amygdale and insula (Damasio, 2003). The brain's "mirror neurons" in the prefrontal cortex may be an essential component in the brain's capacity to imagine another person's perspective and to empathize.

REFERENCES

Anderson, L. W., & Krathwohl, D. R. (Eds.). (2001). *A taxonomy for learning, teaching, and assessing: A revision of Bloom's taxonomy of educational objectives.* New York: Addison Wesley Longman.

Bandler, R., & Grinder, J. (1979). *Frogs into princes: Neuro linguistic programming.* Moab, UT: Real People Press.

Binet, A., & Simon, T. (1916). *The development of intelligence in children.* Baltimore: Williams & Wilkens.

Bloom, B. (1956). *Taxonomy of educational objectives.* New York: David McKay.

Cabeza, R., & St. Jacques, P. (2007). Functional neural imaging of autobiographical memory. *Trends in Cognitive Sciences, 11*(5), 219–227.

Cappelletti, M., et al. (2007). rTMS over the intraparietal sulcus disrupts numerosity processing. *Experimental Brian Research, 179*, 631–642.

Cattell, R. B. (1971). *Abilities: Their structure, growth, and action.* Boston: Houghton Mifflin.

Damasio, A. (2003). *Looking for Spinoza: Joy, sorrow, and the feeling brain.* New York: Harcourt.

Douglas Hospital Regional Research Centre, Quebec, Canada. (2002). *Broca's area, Wernicke's area, and other language-processing areas in the brain.* The brain from bottom to top. Retrieved October 15, 2008, from http://thebrain.mcgill.ca

Dunn, R., & Dunn K. (1993). *Teaching secondary students through their individual learning styles.* Boston: Allyn & Bacon.

Dunn, R., Dunn, K., & Price, G. E. (1984). *Learning style inventory.* Lawrence, KS: Price Systems.

Feldman, D. (1998). How spectrum began. In J. Chen, M. Krechevsky, & J. Viens, *Building on children's strengths: The experience of Project Spectrum.* New York: Teachers College Press.

Fernandez-Duque, D., Baird, J. A., & Posner, M. I. (2000). Executive attention and metacognitive regulation. *Consciousness and Cognition, 9,* 288–307.

Gaffin, D., & Haywood, C. (1993). A spurious category-specific visual agnosia for living things in normal human and nonhuman primates. *Journal of Cognitive Neuroscience, 5,* 118–128.

Galton, F. (1883). *Inquiries into human faculty and its development.* New York: Macmillan.

Gardner, H. (1993). *Frames of mind: The theory of Multiple Intelligences* (rev. ed.). New York: Basic Books.

Gardner, H. (1999). *Intelligence reframed: Multiple intelligences for the 21st century.* New York: Basic Books.

Gazzaniga, M. (1999). (Ed.). Computational motor control. *The cognitive neurosciences.* Cambridge, MA: MIT Press.

Goleman, D. (1995). *Emotional intelligence.* New York: Bantam Books.

Goleman, D. (2006). *Social intelligence: The new science of human relationships.* NY: Bantam.

Guilford, J. P. (1954). *The nature of human intelligence.* New York: McGraw-Hill.

Hafting, T. (2005, August). Microstructure of a spatial map in the entorhinal cortex. *Nature, 436,* 801–806.

Herrnstein, R., & Murray, C. (1994). *The bell curve: Intelligence and class structure in American life.* New York: The Free Press.

Horn, J. L. (1967). Age differences in fluid and crystallized intelligence. *Acta Psychologica, 26*(2), 107–129.

Jung, C. G. (1969). *Psychology and education.* Princeton, NJ: Princeton University Press.

Keirsy, D., & Bates, M. (1984). *Please understand me: Character and temperament types.* Del Mar, CA: Prometheus Nemesis.

Koelsch, S., Kritz, T., Schulze, F., Alsop, D., & Schlaug, D. (2005). Adults and children processing music: An fMRI study. *NeuroImage, 25,* 1068–1076.

Kolb, D. (1985). *Learning style inventory.* Boston, MA: McBer.

Noble, T. (2004). Integrating the revised Bloom's taxonomy with multiple intelligences: A planning tool for curriculum differentiation. *Teachers College Record, 106*(1), 193–211.

Perez, I., & Gagnon, I. (1999). Dissociation between recognition and emotional judgment for melodies. *Neurocase, 5,* 21–30.

Piaget, J. (1950). *The psychology of intelligence.* London: Routledge, Kegan & Paul.

Posner, M. I., & Rothbart, M. K. (2007). Research on attention networks as a model for integration of psychological science. *Annual Review of Psychology 58,* 1–23.

Salovey, P., & Mayer, J. D. (1990). Emotional intelligence. *Imagination, Cognition, and Personality, 9,* 185–211.

Schlaug, G. L., Jancke, Y., & Steinmetz, H. (1995). In vivo evidence of structure brain asymmetry in musicians. *Science, 267,* 699–701.

Shearer, C. B. (2006). *Towards an integrated model of triarchic and multiple intelligences.* Retrieved January 15, 2009, from http://www.miresearch.org/reports_and_papers.html

Silver, H. F., Strong, R. W., & Perini, M. (2000). *So each may learn: Integrating learning styles and multiple intelligences.* Alexandra, VA: ASCD.

Spearman, C. (1927). *The abilities of man*. New York: MacMillan.

Sperry, R. (1961). Cerebral organization and behavior. *Science*, *133*, 1749–1757.

Sternberg, R. (1997). *Thinking styles*. Cambridge, UK: Cambridge University Press.

Sternberg, R., et al. (1996). Identification, instruction, and assessment of gifted children: A construct validation of a triarchic model. *Gifted Child Quarterly*, *40*, (3).

Sternberg, R. J. (1985). *Beyond IQ: The triarchic theory of human intelligence*. New York: Cambridge University Press.

Terman, L. M. (1921). Intelligence and its measurement. *Journal of Educational Psychology*, *12*, 128–133.

Thurstone, L. L. (1938). *Primary mental abilities*. Chicago: University of Chicago Press.

Wechsler, D. (1958). *The measurement and appraisal of adult intelligence*. Baltimore: Williams & Wilkins.

CHAPTER 2

A Conversation About Multiple Intelligences

An Interview with Noam Chomsky

Branton Shearer: Can you reflect on similarities between your work and the theory of multiple intelligences?

Noam Chomsky: My views from the beginning of my work in the 1950s were that the mind is very much like the rest of the organism. It's a modular structure. If you look at the body below the neck you have various subsystems: digestive, visual, immune system, et cetera. They each have their own fairly well integrated internal properties. Of course, they're not totally independent from each other. They share properties, but they have an internal cohesion. This is what we try to grasp when we look at them as individual "organs" of the body. *Organs* might be a loose term but not a vacuous one. They interact within the life of the organism, but are still distinct from each other. My suspicion is that our mental faculties function pretty much the same way.

I discussed this in detail in my book *Reflections on Language* (1975), which proposes that there are a variety of modules in the mind each with its partially distinct structure. Language is one of them. "Theory of mind" is another possible module that is now being extensively researched. Moral faculties are also being investigated. Probably we have special "science forming" faculties that are particular ways of investigating the world that lead us to acquiring and having confidence in scientific knowledge. There are probably a variety of others. These modular systems have some things in common but each has its own structure. When the organism is presented with the data of life the organism turns that data into "experience" by analysis through the various modules of mind and then they operate on that interpreted experience, yielding an array of cognitive competences. This is similar in spirit to Howard's multiple intelligences theory, but he identified types of intelligence and capacities of mind. MI theory is compatible with and similar in spirit to my own formulation, but not identical. I didn't try to identify seven types of intelligence as he did.

BS: Each intelligence has its own symbol system for communication. Can you reflect on any similarities between MI theory and your work in linguistics, particularly, "deep" and "surface" structures?

NC: The technical terms *deep* and *surface* structure have specific meanings in the study of language, but they also have an informal intuitive meaning. A transcription of a conversation that can be read and understood by someone else is an example of surface evidence of a communication. Underlying that surface structure are processes of interpretation, analysis, and integration of meaning with our other experiences and thought which are partially shared between us. Actually, considerably shared or else we wouldn't be able to communicate. These "deep structures," as we might call them informally, are internal to us and have their own properties. Parts of that process are what you call deep structure. They aren't visible on the surface. You have to discover them, for example, in the way that you discover the workings of the visual system. If you see a cube rotating in space, you have a surface perception. Something is happening on the retina. What appears on the retina is a two-dimensional image but it can be presented in such a way that it will be interpreted as a three-dimensional cube rotating in space. This is because of internal processes and analysis that interpret the lines. There are other possible interpretations, but we are compelled by the nature of our visual system to try to interpret it as the motions of a rigid object. Those internal systems are analogous to "deep structure."

I presume that every aspect of our thought, action, and planning have similar properties, if we could ever discover them.

BS: This would include the workings for each of the multiple intelligences. Your work in linguistics challenged the existing models of language and accepted methods of doing science. Do you think Howard's approach to intelligence did the same thing in 1983?

NC: When I started doing research in the 1950s the prevailing scientific methodology was collecting and organizing data on behavior. I adopted what I consider to be a more conservative approach (as opposed to the radical behaviorism that dominated), which employs data as evidence for understanding the internal mechanisms that yield behavior.

The data are not the focus of attention in and of themselves. They are something that you hope to turn into evidence—and *evidence* is a relational term—for or against some theoretical explanatory system for understanding and determining the inner mechanisms that underlie the data. This is a standard model for science and suggesting that human sciences or the sciences of understanding animals adopt this model is not all that radical.

BS: You might consider this conservative, but it was in direct opposition to the field at the time. Howard's proposal of MI theory has also challenged prevailing scientific methodology and conceptions of intelligence. It harkens back to a time before behaviorism and empiricism dominated.

NC: I think my work and Howard's have been part of a wave in the shift in perspective from the focus on attention on behavior and its products to understanding the inner mechanisms that give rise to behavior. That's what led to the cognitive sciences. This has come to be known as the "cognitive revolution." Howard's work is part of that general shift in conception of how we should study thought and action. He was saying that particular measures of language facility or arithmetic skill (like IQ tests) are only touching on the "surface" behavior and not telling us much about the organization of intelligence.

BS: Do you think it is true that multiple intelligences gives us a powerful tool to better describe how we solve problems and think in everyday life?

NC: It gets away from the rigid and rather arid measures that may have their uses to predict certain performances like achievement in the first year of college or something like that. But they do not give insight and understanding into how well people deal with other people, et cetera, and all the other important aspects of everyday life.

Multiple intelligences theory is exploring new terrain and so has met with a certain amount of resistance. This is in part because each of the theoretically proposed intelligences is difficult to study. They are shaped differently from traditional conceptions of intelligence, and ideas about them are hard to verify. It is hard enough to study the inner mechanisms of insect behavior, and so with humans it is qualitatively more complex. All such work is going to be exploratory and properly subjected to qualifications and alternative explanations, et cetera. Such debates in science can be quite healthy.

BS: It is a healthy scientific debate if people are informed and open, but there can be an emotional barrier to accepting a new idea like MI. People have a lot invested in IQ—both personally as well as professionally.

NC: This is true for all the sciences, but it may be particularly true for the human sciences. The barriers are very high. Such resistance is not unknown in the physical sciences, however. Take molecular theory, for example. A century ago that idea was considered at best controversial and at worst ridiculous. Leading scientists like Poincaré said that the only reason we pay attention to the molecular theory of gases was because we were familiar with the game of billiards. Ludwig Boltzmann, who created much of molecular theory, committed suicide apparently in part because he felt that he couldn't convince people to take molecular theory seriously.

I think it is still premature to call MI a mature "scientific theory." It is a viable framework for approaching the question of how to develop significant theories of human thought and intelligence. This is a task which is a long ways off. It is immense task. In fact, even in narrower areas such as linguistics, which is an aspect of intelligence (and is more easily isolatable), I am reluctant to talk about it in terms of a "theory" in the sense that it is used in the natural sciences. In MI and linguistics there are frameworks for theories, models, and so on.

BS: Fully mature scientific theories have yet to be formulated.

NC: In order to move this project forward we need to study in as much depth as possible the most promising particular candidates for modules of mind: language, moral judgment, theory of mind, et cetera. Neuroscience evidence should be explored as fully as possible but it's very difficult for ethical reasons, especially for humans. It is easier to do neurological studies with animals and much has been learned from this work, but it is impossible with humans because it is unethical. Of course, some invasive research has been done with humans in the past and much has been learned from it, but it's not possible today. This is important because a great deal of human intelligence appears to be species specific so there is often no significant comparative evidence from other species. This seriously reduces the ability to investigate the neurological bases of human intelligence. Of course, there are some technological advances that have made it possible to conduct some noninvasive studies that give some evidence into what is going on in the brain but it's an extremely difficult topic to take on. In a way it's rather like cosmology. You cannot do the experiments *directly;* you can only look at data developed by sophisticated experimentations to give some interpretation of it that makes sense.

The definition of *intelligence* [see Chapter 1] used in MI theory can be described as a "persuasive definition," which makes sense. This is not so much a definition in the technical sense as a proposal of how we should look at the questions. It's a proposal that says, Let's look at the questions that fall under the loose rubric of *intelligence* in terms of a broader criteria such as value to a community. That's a suggestion that is valuable so far as it inspires inquiry which leads to deeper understanding. This proposal challenges a very narrow sense of science that says that we should simply consider the properties of the individual abstracted from the community setting in which she or he functions.

BS: MI defines intelligence as being contextually based using materials pertinent to each intelligence. It also includes the creation of things and the providing of valuable services. Is this problematic? Many people don't seem to understand this basic definition or simply reject it out of hand.

NC: One can quibble about whether or not you should call that "intelligence" but it carves out an area of inquiry that places the individual in the context of communal interaction and the creation and adherence to values. That's a valid topic to study and it's not unfair to call it an aspect of intelligence.

This approach to intelligence isn't particularly difficult to understand but some people may reject it simply because they're not interested in it. Or maybe they reject MI because they don't think this is the correct way to study this scientific question. All research, no matter what it is, it may be physics or whatever, is guided by maybe an imprecise or perhaps unconscious conception of the way we think the world is going to work. These research intuitions are certainly subject to challenge. Some turn out to be useful and some turn out to be wrong.

BS: So after 25 years is the jury still out on the viability of MI theory?

NC: Yes, given that there are dissension and vocal critics, but my guess is that something similar to MI theory will crystallize and become a kind of scientific norm in the future—some kind of modularity of mental faculties and their relation to larger interactions among humans. It may be that at least in certain areas the most productive way to investigate broader interactions between the mind and the outside world (including other people) is to concentrate on the inner mechanisms themselves. This is another research intuition that may be tested in the future.

BS: So a problem is that research into MI theory has been limited because of the lack of equipment and assessment technology?

NC: Yes. Take, for example, graduate education, where you learn techniques and the appropriate technology within a field. You do a thesis within a theoretical framework that is pretty well set in place. It is sometimes fairly straightforward to apply technology that you worked hard to acquire and then you can spend the rest of your life applying that in slightly different conditions and situations. On the other hand, trying to explore a domain where the techniques and technology haven't really been refined is a lot harder. There's much greater risk of failure. If you apply techniques that you have learned to some new situation you're likely to find something at least. . . . It may not be of any particular value but you will have found something. On the other hand, if you're exploring an area where the technology has not been refined you may find yourself just up against a blank wall or you may make a *real* discovery.

BS: Do you think that MI theory has made a valuable contribution to the conversation about how best to design schools and how to teach?

NC: In the area of education and teaching there are two ideals or extremes. At the one extreme the goal is for students to obtain a high score on a test. This is exemplified by the No Child Left Behind Act, where we teach to the test. The other extreme is a more traditional view from the 18th century where the goal—paraphrasing from the tradition—isn't to pour liquid into a vessel but instead to lay out a thread that the learner may proceed along in his or her own way. This approach emphasizes discovering knowledge rather than acquiring something that is poured inside. Those are very different ideas about teaching. My own view is that the testing model is terrible. It's merely training for obedience and subordination and mechanical performance. It undermines creativity and the capacity for constructive social interaction and so on.

We've all had the experience of studying hard to pass an exam and then two weeks later forgetting everything that we learned. This happens because that kind of instruction isn't coming from within. It is being imposed from without. It just doesn't last. It's a terrible model. It only makes sense if we want to train people to be in the Marine Corps or factory workers.

BS: It's not a model for the 21st century that we want to follow as a national model. In fact, the best forms of education don't work that way.

NC: We've developed over the years a two-tier system of education. For mass education, the emphasis is on training, obedience, rote skills, and subordination. A different kind of schooling that encourages creativity and independence of thought is offered for the privileged few. At a place like MIT, an elite, largely graduate science university, students don't go to class to listen to lectures and take notes and pass tests. Students are expected to challenge the instruction. One professor was famous for his answer to freshman students who asked, "What are we going to cover in this class?" His routine answer was, "It doesn't matter what we cover. It matters what we *discover* along the way." I think that's the right model for education.

BS: This is embedded in MI theory. Can an MI perspective help to bring this approach to mass education (not just the elite) by recognizing and valuing the unique MI strengths of all *students?*

NC: One of the greatest graduate courses I ever had in math was one in which the instructor would come into the room and write something on the blackboard—a possible theorem. He'd look at it in a puzzled way and then he'd turn to the class and say, "Now let's see if that's really a theorem or if it's false." And then the students would have suggestions on how to approach it. Try this, try that. There would be interaction. It was a guided process. If it was going off track he'd suggest something else. By the end of the class we'd be able to say, "Well, here's the proof for it." It's that kind of instruction that you remember. You don't simply memorize to answer a test question and then forget it. It gives you an internalized mode of discovery and creativity. It is hard to put your finger on this process but it becomes part of you. It is thinking that is revealed.

BS: It is participatory and engaged. It reveals how people can solve important problems in daily life—plumbers, skilled craftspeople, and the like.

NC: If MI theory can give people a powerful language to describe our thinking in everyday life then it has made a real contribution. I am amazed watching skilled craftsmen and the kinds of problems that they can solve that appear unsolvable to me. How they plunge in and solve them.

BS: An MI model of intelligence values this diversity of abilities so that it's not just academic achievement that is celebrated or valued in the classroom. We all have those places where our unique forms of intelligence work the best. The challenge is finding those places where we each can fit.

NC: Needless to say, life consists of a lot more than meeting classroom goals. And facing life's challenges and opportunities calls upon many kinds of cognitive capacities, on multiple intelligences. Discovery of their types, their functioning, and the inner mechanisms that enter into their use is a demanding task for the study of thought and action, now barely within the grasp of serious inquiry.

REFERENCE

Chomsky, N. (1975). *Reflections on language.* New York: Pantheon Books.

Neuroscience and Multiple Intelligences Theory: Barriers and Bridges?

An Interview with Marc Hauser

Branton Shearer: Marc, can you talk a little about your understanding of multiple intelligences and its relationship to your work as a scientist?

Marc Hauser: A long time ago in the 1980s when I was in graduate school I heard Howard Gardner speak. At the time I was deeply steeped in the theoretical framework of brain modularity and, in particular, the notion of domain specificity. I was influenced by the work of Chomsky, Fodor, and many others in the cognitive sciences with a nativist bias. One of the reasons why it was easy for me to slide into this tradition was that it was simpatico with my background in biology and, especially, the tradition of ethology as developed by Lorenz, Tinbergen, and von Frisch.

When I first heard about MI theory I was not attracted to it. I had rejected the idea of intelligence itself because it seemed too fuzzy a concept for scientific research. As such, the idea of multiple *intelligences* didn't clarify things. I have spent most of my career studying animals. It is an incoherent question to ask if animals have intelligence. In my popular book, *Wild Minds* (2000), I did not even use the word *intelligence*, because it doesn't make any sense. If you want to understand the psychology of animals as well as humans then you have to ask questions where you can be precise. For example, you might ask, Does an animal have the ability to make a representation of a symbol? Can they use this representation to navigate within an environment? Can they use symbols to compute various kinds of mathematical operations? The precision is important, and so too it is important to break down rather large conceptual domains into more manageable pieces.

Thus, in the same way that I don't think you can really ask about the evolution of intelligence, I don't think you can ask about the evolution of language or whether animals have language, in part because language isn't a monolithic thing. We can, however, ask questions like, Do animals have the capacity to extract computations that are part of grammatical structure? Can they compute abstract notions of identity? At the end of the day, if you want to say, "That's an *intelligent* animal," fine! But, that's not how I frame the questions.

I'm a nativist, which means I believe that humans, and all other animals, are equipped with neural machinery designed to build particular systems of knowledge about the world, and this machinery constrains the format of their knowledge as well as what is acquired over development. This is a perspective that has motivated considerable work in biology and has played an important role in the cognitive revolution.

Returning to the main theme, and my background, because ethologists think about brain/mind specializations for solving certain kinds of problems, it was natural to gravitate toward Chomsky and Fodor. In contrast, the notion of multiple intelligences, though potentially appealing to different kinds of knowledge and expertise, was premised on a more experiential or constructed view of such systems. Thus, for example, my students and I have applied the domain-specificity perspective to problems of language evolution, music, morality, and mathematics. Our investigations explore questions such as, What are the principles that organize the kind of knowledge humans have of language and music; are the principles of organization entirely separate or shared in some way, and to what extent are the principles uniquely human or shared with other animals? Are the mechanisms that enable acquisition of native moral systems similar to or different from those enabling acquisition of subsequent moral systems?

These specific kinds of scientific questions haven't been broached by the field of multiple intelligences. As such, MI theory hasn't been applicable to any of the research in animal cognition, or the kind of cognitive neuroscience that I, and many others work on.

There is, however, one recent problem that my students and I have explored, where an MI view might be relevant. In particular, we have been looking at the problem of general intelligence or IQ in animals, and in particular, a small nonhuman primate called the cotton-top tamarin monkey. The question here is, What, in a broad sense, makes human intelligence unique? I used to think that there were quite striking parallels between human and nonhuman animal thought. But I now think that the differences are quite significant. In particular, and relevant to the notion of specialized intelligence, I think that animals have "laser beam" intelligence, that is, a highly specialized ability to solve ecologically and socially relevant problems in a precise way. But what they don't have is a more "floodlight" kind of intelligence—the ability to recruit other laser beams to solve new kinds of problems. My favorite hypothesis is that humans have uniquely evolved capacities that allow integration across domains of knowledge, yielding what some call *general intelligence*. You can call this either little *g*, IQ, or multiple intelligences. Either way, we have this unique capacity to integrate across systems, which gives us a specialized capacity that other animals lack.

This idea can apply in either a unitary or a multiple intelligences perspective. People who are socially adept have the capacity to recruit knowledge from different domains in the service of social skills in the way that, for example, an autistic child doesn't. Birds have the capacity to hide their seeds and then months later retrieve them. They have a kind of episodic type of memory for finding food that is locked into *that* task. It does not generalize, or perhaps more conservatively, nothing suggests that it does. Animals are locked into specific kinds of knowledge that cannot be recruited for different kinds of tasks—they simply cannot generalize across domains of knowledge in the way that humans can.

BS: What do you think about Howard's description of the neural correlates of each intelligence that he sketched out 25 years ago? Do these still apply today, given the vast advances in the neurosciences?

MH: At this point in time there is a huge gap between the kind of theorizing that goes on in the mind sciences and the neurobiological mechanisms that back it up. Some research indicates that the evidence for specificity of function for neural structures is growing weaker. Different areas of the brain can be recruited to do different tasks.

Of course, we know there are direct relationships between mind and brain, but we're a long way from knowing much about how the brain affects the mind, especially in the areas where we create theories about mental states. When it comes to asking about the neural correlates of cognitive function, we are, therefore, in a primitive phase, forced to ask about general correlations. Is there a connection between IQ and frontal lobe functions? Well, yes, but what does this mean either in terms of the representation of IQ in the brain or in regard to the mechanisms that subserve the construction or acquisition of intelligences? Further, since the frontal lobes are recruited for a lot of other things such as emotions and decision making, working memory, et cetera, we can't make any progress in understanding neural mechanisms *for* IQ.

BS: One function of MI theory is to serve as a bridge between our understanding of the mind/brain and teaching and the design of education. What's your opinion?

MH: I think there is a significant gap between what we're learning in the mind/brain sciences and what's happening in the schools. There are interesting and exciting conferences on brain and education that focus on this topic, but the gap is still very wide. I don't think that people in the educational trenches take the information emerging from the cognitive and neural sciences into their classrooms. This may, in part, be because of poor packaging on the part of scientists, but I think it is more likely due to the fact that the discoveries don't, in any significant way, have much bearing yet on education. There are no clues, in most cases, for ameliorating education, improving learning, attention, motivation. Though I've gone to my daughters' schools to share my research on the brain, and enjoyed myself each time, I don't think that the students really profit, and nor do I think that the teachers benefit in terms of integrating the material into their curriculum.

MI may well be doing a better job here, but I am not aware of this. When I have approached educators to discuss theories of knowledge acquisition, conceptual change, knowledge representations, and brain plasticity, it is of academic interest, but seems impenetrable in terms of applied problems. I think this is unfortunate, but don't have any good suggestions for bringing the groups together, except to go beyond the conference and book format, to forging direct collaborative efforts.

BS: MI theory strives to serve as a bridge between people's understanding of the mind/brain and what they can do with this information. One function that it serves is to inform people (teachers and parents and students) of the uniqueness of each individual student. By understanding that each child has a unique profile of MI strengths and limitations then they can be taught differently. An MI assessment helps with this endeavor.

MH: The study of individual differences has so far been a very small segment of the cognitive neuroscience research agenda. The emphasis has been on describing what is "universal" about people rather than what is unique about each person. But I think that interest in this topic is increasing as relatively inexpensive neuroimaging tools and techniques are now more available. Researchers are starting to report and discuss somewhat larger scale studies that describe individual variability in neuroanatomy and how it maps onto concepts such as IQ.

For example, Paul Thompson at UCLA has investigated variation in frontal lobe volume relative to IQ. Walter Mischel at Columbia has looked at delayed gratification or patience and its relationship to future performance variables such as grades in high school, juvenile delinquency, and even marital stability. But for the most part, many of us in the cognitive and neurosciences have looked for group effects and universal patterns, or what is common to our species, riding over any potential individual differences.

BS: Of course, when it comes to teaching and learning you also need to know what's different or unique about each student.

MH: I think that you need to understand both—what's universal in child development as well as individual uniqueness. For example, it is interesting to know that most kids at about the age of four will have an appreciation for the goals, beliefs, and tendencies of other people—interpersonal awareness. Let me emphasize the word *most* here, as of course there is some variation. But to a large extent, this looks very much like a maturational process that is, to some extent, immune to variation in developmental experiences. From a more applied perspective, the notion of milestones for particular developmental achievements can have negative consequences for many parents, as they set up expectations for their children. If the child fails to achieve the milestone on the designated date, they panic. Here, education for parents is central.

BS: This is different from MI, which sees each intelligence as "skill" or competence that we each have developed at differing levels rather than as merely an unfolding process of maturation that is equally shared by everyone.

MH: That is absolutely right. From the nativist perspective, there are core competences that everyone has at the start. Individual differences arise in performance and can certainly be accounted for by aspects of experience. I think what you perceive as a difference has less to do with maturation versus skill development than with the kinds of questions that are of interest. Thus, the nativist would want to know what the starting state of knowledge looks like, how the machinery that underpins this system guides and constrains subsequent change, and this, in turn, would give some picture of the range of potential variation in what you or MI theorists might want to call differences in skill.

BS: What are your thoughts on the role and impact of MI on mind/brain/education?

MH: Overall, I think that MI has played an important role in getting educators off the myopic focus on a certain kind of intelligence. It has been a healthy strategy in this regard for educators. Concerning my own scientific research, it hasn't played much of a role except perhaps in how MI can get mapped onto different domains of knowledge. I'm not sure if this is a fair mapping, but Gardner has in the past talked about brain "modules."

BS: Doesn't MI simply provide a broad framework for understanding specific sets of skills and abilities that are the same as the "domain specific capacities" that your research investigates?

MH: I don't think Howard's notion of "skill" really maps on to the notion of "domain-specific competence." Skill implies, at least on a folk view, some kind of capacity that you work on to improve, like learning to play chess, play tennis, do long division, and so forth. In contrast, the domain-specificity view speaks to a set of core systems of knowledge that all members of a species will have, and that set the stage (and constrain) subsequent acquisition. In this sense, the tradition that comes from the computational view of the mind raises different kinds of questions that may or may not be compatible with an MI perspective.

MI has had a different agenda as a theory from that of my work on domain specificity and neuroscience. They share the view that the mind/ brain is not one big general function processing system. We share that view very strongly and anyone today who still thinks that is simply wrong, given what we know.

But there are also big differences. Our approaches differ in regard to their mission. I think that MI sees its role mainly as an educational theory to promote real-world learning rather than as a theoretical framework for understanding how the brain works.

BS: The definition that Howard uses to identify each intelligence may also present problems for its use as a neuroscientific theory: "a set of skills or abilities that allows a person to solve a problem or fashion a product that is valued by at least one culture." This is a big *definition that has some important implications for what do you in the realm of teaching and learning, but it may be problematic for informing neuroscience research. This definition includes the logical problem solving like IQ but it goes on from there to include creative abilities and contextually based performances. Researching "contextual and creative thinking" is difficult. Also, many people in the research world either do not understand this definition or simply do not accept it, so the conversation stops there. There are also problems in furthering an MI research agenda because there aren't good assessment tools for researchers to use. This has limited MI impact on the neuroscience field. What do you think of the future for MI theory?*

MH: There are many people investigating the mind/brain/education connections, for example, at Harvard, where Howard and I both teach, but at many other institutions as well. Many students are researching basic mind/ brain questions, but there is little focus on curriculum and instruction. Of course, some people are looking at areas such as the neuroscience of reading, but a lot of this work is not very practical. Much of this research is still very theoretical and not applicable to teachers in the classroom.

We probably should really sit down and discuss why the gap between neuroscience and education is still so wide and what to do about it in our research agendas.

BS: One answer to that question is "assessment" that describes the differences between students so you can see them happening in the classroom and address them in your instruction and curriculum. The "So what?" question is huge. How do we help people to understand themselves—their intrapersonal intelligence— so that they can be more successful? Can we help them to recruit their MI strengths to enhance learning? Can we enhance motivation for learning?

MH: That reminds me that this past term I taught one of the most exciting courses I've ever taught at Harvard titled Consumable Science. It was a new course that addressed the need to improve scientific literacy in the world. We tried to address the question, Why aren't people more literate about science? The goal of the course was to excite students to form an organization or company with the mission of changing the face of science in the public. The problem isn't a lack of materials about science, but rather a "one size fits all" approach to teaching science that has failed. We need to take a fresh took and find out why children—who are initially very excited about science—stop loving science. Why? It can be boring! We have a lot of bad teaching approaches that are myopic, with a lot of repetition and too much focus on the text. Why can't we use interesting stories to teach science? Why not movies? Why not music or theater?

We have a lot of science information and materials that are text based and for a lot of students they're boring. It's always the same mode. What we need are hard-hitting activities that grab people and engage them and show them that they are missing out. We need to make it cool. We need to grab them with hip-hop lyrics, movies, documentaries. The goal is to engage them. People are going to get sucked in for different reasons. You have to make them comfortable and help them to own the material. How do you do that?

BS: I think that you engage them by addressing their MI strengths.

MH: Indeed. Are you familiar with Ira Glass's radio program, *This American Life*? Ira Glass sometimes tells some magical stories about science. He sneaks science learning in there and it really grabs people. It's not for all people, but you will capture some portion of the population that you wouldn't otherwise.

BS: Your class reminds me that MI also strives to build a bridge between "science" and "art." It is inherent in the very MI definition of what it means to be intelligent in the world, but it is also there in the "So what?" question about teaching. Discoveries about the science of the human/mind/brain can help us to know how to engage learners actively in the learning process—as creators. I don't think that this has been very well articulated so we are left with this dichotomy— you are either doing the soft work of teaching or the hard science. We have had difficulty building a bridge to mend that gap as a legitimate "scientific enterprise." My work has been in using an MI assessment to build connections between the neurocognitive sciences and the identification of student strengths and the art of teaching. Your story about how you engaged your class with many different intelligences and at a high level of creativity illustrates how this can work beautifully.

MH: I agree.

BS: To summarize, the idea of multiple intelligences is too general and vague to be useful in cognitive neuroscience research, but neuroscience researchers such as yourself are identifying cerebral structures related to many of the intelligences, for example, musical ability, interpersonal perspective taking, logical reasoning, and self awareness, in both humans and animals.

Science research has avoided using the terminology of MI, but there has been work establishing a relationship between some IQ-related skills and neural structures.

A major barrier between MI and neuroscience is that they ask different kinds of questions and thus don't intersect in the minds of most researchers. Another limitation is the scientific tradition that focuses on finding "universal" laws about human behavior/biology, and most researchers view MI as more of an "applied" theory useful for describing individual differences rather than as a universal description of human abilities.

In your view, the future for MI is brighter for MI as a powerful "educational theory" that moves educators beyond IQ rather than as a neuroscientific framework for understanding mind/brain functions.

REFERENCE

Hauser, M. (2000). *Wild minds: What animals really think.* New York: Henry Holt.

CHAPTER 4

Neuroscience and the Multiple Intelligences: Advances Since 1983

Michael Posner

There have been a lot of neuroscience advances in the past 25 years since MI theory was introduced. I am an admirer of Gardner's contribution but I don't think it had much direct influence on neuroscience. MI and neuroscience developed pretty much independently of each other. What was different about Gardner was his effort to connect intelligence and neuropsychology. This was a good idea that is likely to remain important for future efforts. Another basic test of multiple intelligences is in the field of education and whether or not it helps educators to train children and help them to develop.

The dialogue has changed since 1983. It is difficult to say exactly which changes in the field are attributable to MI, which to neuroimaging or to genetics research. Much of Gardner's original research was based on lesion data (brain injury) and could easily be dismissed as not relevant to normal function. Neuroimaging has changed that; it clearly deals with normal function.

Neuroscience has accepted plasticity much more over the past 20 years. Much of this change results from the research of Michael Merzenich (Merzenich & Kaas, 1982) but Gardner was correct in linking brain function to intelligence and thus to learning and plasticity. I think neuroimaging has shown clearly that different brain networks underlie the forms of intelligence that Gardner proposed. When it is more completely recognized that the efficiency of these networks differ among people Gardner's idea will have a very firm basis in cognitive neuroscience.

Gardner made a neuroscientific argument for MI theory that was based largely, but not entirely, on lesion data. Of course, there's a cultural overlay to the concept of intelligence as well. Since 1983 there have evolved many more techniques and much research that has suggested that, first, there are a variety of skills that are based on distinct neural networks, some of them overlapping. We have much better knowledge of these neural networks described by MI theory since Gardner wrote *Frames of Mind*. Also, the efficiency of the networks differ among people—partly for genetic reasons. These same genes are important in the development of these networks. Human efficiency varies partly from differences in these genes and partly from the experiences of the individual. There is an interaction between the two. Those findings have given a better underpinning for the argument that there are neural bases for each of the intelligences.

The intelligences that Gardner described in 1983 are a good way of summarizing some of the networks that have been studied by neuroscientists since then. But I don't think there has been a comprehensive review of the of the neuroscience research data relating to each of the multiple intelligences since Gardner's original writing. But some of my research into individual differences (Posner & Rothbart, 2007a, 2007b) and the neuroimaging studies of other scientists certainly pertain to it.

I've been involved with a group that is studying the educational influences of arts training. That is a very good vehicle for understanding the networks that underlie each intelligence and how some people learn very quickly, others with more difficulty, and some not at all in arts areas related to each intelligence.

It would be a worthy project for someone steeped in MI theory to go through all the neural networks that have been associated with each of the multiple intelligences and review the research data since 1983. It would be a big job, but it could be done.

The people who should be most interested in this kind of project are the new mind-brain-education centers that have recently been established at several large research universities such as Harvard, Cambridge, and Vanderbilt. These programs need to establish links between curricular suggestions such as those based on MI and brain systems, and such a project would be an excellent step.

There's a long history in psychology of trying to organize intelligence into subcategories. For example, Guilford's model describes more than 120 intelligences, and Sternberg's Triarchic theory includes three types of intelligence. Their popularity comes and goes. Sternberg's three intelligences (creativity, practical, and analytical) subsume a vast array of subskills, and whether there are good reasons for collecting them all together is debatable. It makes a nice book, but his are very general categories and I don't know where you go to take them into the domain of brain activity.

MI theory has run into trouble gaining acceptance because of the No Child Left Behind (NCLB) law, which emphasizes a few common skills. This is very different from the direction you think about with multiple intelligences that values an array of individual differences. If a child isn't strong in the few selected skills (reading and math, for example) then he or she is at a disadvantage even though possibly being very good at something else. MI has great difficulty being accepted in the NCLB school environment.

The NCLB outcome tests make it more difficult to cater to the individual's particular learning skills. It's possible, but it's more difficult, because you have to get everyone up to a standard at a given moment regardless of a person's developmental uniqueness. The idea of teaching that accounts for the multiple intelligences profiles of students gets lost in the conversation. The emphasis is all on the test results—outcome measures—and not on how best to help children to learn skills and develop their potential.

Neuroimaging is generally supportive of the direction of MI theory, but MI as such hasn't been accepted because the data hasn't been gathered together as an empirical test of the theory's predictions. I think some of this is happening, however, in various research initiatives. One of the best examples is in reading research (Posner & Rothbart, 2007a, Chap. 7). The methodology used in reading research could be applied to any of the topics that MI theory covers. Most of the intelligences have been addressed to some degree by neuroscience. For example, we have descriptions of the networks underpinning emotional intelligence, somatosensory intelligence, and so on, but I think in reading there has been more of an emphasis on individual differences than in the other areas. Investigating the neurological differences in individuals with differing levels of skill is relevant to the question of intelligence. Reading research and recently arithmetic research have also examined the neural bases of individual skill differences (Posner & Rothbart, 2007a, Chap. 8). I think that all the different intelligences will probably be studied in the future.

One big development in neuroscience for understanding individual differences is in the area of studying connectivity within networks. Researchers look at the strength by which one node in a neural network activates another node in that network. This is a very good way to understand a range of individual differences by describing where the differences are manifesting themselves in the neural networks and how they might change with experiences. This is part of the efficiency argument. Greater skill level and learning speed is indicated by greater efficiency and connectivity.

The study of expertise is one way of examining the efficiency of particular networks and how the nodes change with practice. A reduction in the extent of neural activation often accompanies greater expertise. The study of connectivity is crucial because when you become efficient you get very strong relations between particular nodes so the overall activation becomes less but their communication is better. The focalization of activation between particular nodes is common in many skills and is accompanied by better transmission of information and communication among these nodes.

This fits very well with the idea of Hebb (1949, 1966) that every psychological event, sensation, expectation, emotion, or thought is represented by the flow of activity in a set of interconnected neurons. Hebb attempted to provide a fully integrated psychology that applied his neural network theory to many functional areas, including emotions, in their social contexts learning and individual differences in intelligence (see also Posner & Rothbart, 2007b). MI theory should be aligned with this work.

I think there is a future for MI theory as a way to understand individual differences. I don't know if the name *multiple intelligences* will be used, but it is important to understand the neuroscience of individuals. That may produce a way to describe how learning takes place differently in children with particular skill sets and how they improve the functioning of their neural networks in perhaps unique ways.

REFERENCES

Hebb, D. O. (1949). *Organization of behavior*. New York: John Wiley & Sons.

Hebb, D. O. (1966). *A textbook of psychology* (2nd ed.). Philadelphia: W. B. Saunders.

Merzenich, M. M., & Kaas, J. H. (1982). Reorganization of mammalian somatosensory cortex following peripheral nerve injury. *Trends in Neuroscience, 5*, 434–436.

Posner, M. I., & Rothbart, M. K. (2007a). *Educating the human brain*. Washington, DC: APA Books.

Posner, M. I., & Rothbart, M. K. (2007b). Research on attention networks as a model for the integration of psychological science. *Annual Review of Psychology, 58*, 1–23.

FURTHER READING

Checa, P., Rodriguez-Bailon, R., & Rueda, M. R. (2008). Neurocognitive and temperamental systems of self-regulation and early adolescents' schooling outcomes. *Mind, Brain and Education, 2/4*, 177–186.

Diamond, A., Barnett, S., Thomas, J., & Munro, S. (2007). Preschool improves cognitive control. *Science, 319*, 1185–1186.

Duncan, J., Seitz, R. J., Kolodny, J., Bor, D., Herzon, H., Ahmed, A., Newell, F. N., & Emslie, H. (2000). A neural basis for general intelligence. *Science, 289*, 457–460.

Premack, D., & Premack, A. (2003). *Original Intelligence*. New York: McGraw Hill.

Intrinsic Motivation and Multiple Intelligences

An Interview with Mihaly Csikszentmihalyi

BS: Can you reflect on the relationship with your own work on intrinsic motivation and the impact, status, and future of MI theory?

MC: There hasn't been much attempt to theoretically align MI theory with my work, but a lot of people see them as being complementary. They are trying to institute them at the same time in schools to change things, for example, at the Key Learning Community in Indianapolis and in other schools such as in Denmark. It is also seen as being complementary to the Montessori approach.

There are similarities between MI and my work on intrinsic motivation (1990). They both start with the assumption that people have different sets of skills and the world is full of different opportunities for action. One of the things that educators and parents ought to be concerned about is how to match the skills and unique talents of the individual with the opportunities that are available. If there are no opportunities, then they should create new ones, so that each child has the opportunity to use whatever he or she has. This approach is true both for MI and for how I think about motivation. So it makes sense to integrate my work on motivation with Howard's work that is more cognitive and structural. There is a good synergy between these two basic theories about the development of children.

Howard's MI model has been incredibly successful because it liberates educators from what many of them consider to be a rather constricted and abstract way of imparting knowledge, and also from the kind of knowledge that's being imparted. I think the reason why MI has been so successful is there has been a kind of pent-up frustration on the part of teachers in every industrialized country, that we are not reaching kids all the way. We are only skimming the surface of their abilities and interests. By taking MI into consideration we can be more responsive to each child's abilities. This has made teachers feel empowered in a new way that they weren't before and it has been enormously successful. MI is a very good alternative to the rather staid and abstract form of education that we've been used to.

I also see a kind of limit to MI. It is true that kids like to use their bodies for dance and basketball and such, but in terms of what is the common language of knowledge, it is still true that writing and counting (the linguistic and mathematical skills) are still the lingua franca . . . the gold coin of common currency of educated people. I don't see the possibility of reversing the hegemony of language and numbers in the education system. We have to be much more aware of how to complement those two primary mediums of instruction. We have to be aware that a child needs to use and feel good about the fact that he or she has other abilities . . . such as being socially skilled or visually expressive and all the other intelligences. We need to complement the *master* intelligences of number and language. . . . I think it's going to have a very beneficial effect on education in general.

But some people think that all intelligences are essentially equal. I think that's a mistake because of what society needs and what the culture depends upon. I think society depends on language and numbers more than on movement and the rest.

Sometimes MI is taken to the extreme by teachers assuming that all forms of intelligences should be given equal time in the school. I don't think that's feasible; but who knows, maybe it is.

BS: Do you think that it is a mistake to view MI versus IQ as some sort of revolution? Is it better to see that MI embraces IQ skills and that our understanding of human intelligence is evolving? Would it be helpful to have a model that integrates in teachers' minds IQ with MI?

MC: Yes, of course. People like to set up these dichotomies that one approach is true and another is false. I don't think that this is what Howard intended with MI theory.

It is a problem that we don't have a good way to demonstrate and measure a child's strengths. MI complements my work on intrinsic motivation and in terms of the quality of experience that a child has at any given point in time. The more that education allows people to experience their strongest abilities the better their experience becomes, and thus learning becomes more rewarding. It also makes children's desire to immerse themselves further in learning greater. But I'm not sure whether this leads to greater achievement. That's not my primary concern. I focus on the child's quality of experience in the moment, rather than on his or her accomplishments.

I really think that Howard has made a huge difference in the field of psychology in the sense of humanizing the discipline. For a long time the cognitive sciences, behaviorism, and psychiatry were bound by rather strict orthodoxies. You had a feeling that you had to take a side and they all were very reductionistic and not very interesting. Howard opened up that discourse in ways that hadn't been possible before and that has been very refreshing. His ability to bring the whole artificial intelligence field to the debate has been very interesting historically in terms of the evolution of knowledge. It has been a very good thing, a profoundly enriching influence. I think very highly of everything he does.

I know that there are hard-core psychologists who know only a small part of the discipline and work within a small specialty. Some of them dismiss the more enriching approach that Howard's work represents.

Yes, there is still some question regarding the viability of MI as a "scientific theory," if you mean by it that you can identify the neurological bases of these abilities, or show that, in fact, once you have one of these intelligences activated you will perform better in the predicted direction.

Eventually, these questions will be answered because people will take the trouble to do the work. You need the type of visionary pioneer like Howard to say, Hey, there's a lot of interesting stuff here that we haven't explored yet.

BS: What sort of evidence is necessary to move the discussion along to get out of the IQ-versus-MI debate?

MC: In the society in which we live people who score highly on IQ-type tests do better in school. There's an empirical bit of truth there, but it doesn't tell you if IQ exists or not or where it is located. It just says that if you have the ability to solve the test questions you will be more likely to be successful in our culture.

I don't think that you can develop a test of success that competes with IQ and that will be more valid because of the kind of society that we live in. If we lived in a society where people were highly valued for composing music or jumping high or playing instruments, if that was a condition of success, then an MI-based test would be a more widely adopted measure. We are locked in a particular social situation where to get ahead or succeed in society you need those particular skills that IQ measures.

If, for instance, it were shown that a person who is able to develop his or her gifts in his or her strength area is happier and lives a life that's more content and satisfied, then that would also add to the acceptance of MI.

If people take MI seriously and say, "Yes, I want my children to be happy by doing what they can do best. I would be very happy if someone could tell me what my child's MI potential is. Or perhaps even where my child is lacking something important that will be useful for him or her in later life such as social or intrapersonal intelligence." If someone scores very low on those areas, then that would be a good "ah ha!" because the person will not be able to function very well in society. Why? Because they may not have a good family life or get along well with others. If we could measure that and predict and warn parents that this child needs training or development in a particular intelligence, then that would be much better than an IQ test, which never deals with these issues.

That would make MI more convincing. But for that to happen you need to have a market. It's supply and demand. There is a strong demand for people who can count and write. There is much less demand for people who can jump or sing or be introspective—or even happy.

Another source of evidence for MI would be to identify where each intelligence is located in the brain or what the likelihood is of changing these brain functions. All that is eventually important. But this is different from the popular and society-wide acceptance of the MI concept. To do that you need to change society or at least make a convincing case that children are going to be happier and turn into better-functioning adults.

BS: What are the barriers to MI's playing a stronger role in educational reform?

MC: I don't think any psychological theory is playing a strong role in educational reform. I think that compared with any other theory, MI is doing very well. I think educational reform is driven more by tradition, by financial considerations, by political ideology, and not by science.

BS: So our traditions emphasize testing only for reading and math. MI hasn't affected that tradition.

MC: Yes, these are incredibly difficult institutions to change. Education has an ancient history. The Chinese had sets of tests for officials that haven't changed much in hundreds of years. It's because society doesn't change much basically over time. Society is still rewarding more or less the same skills that it did during the Renaissance, when Western schools were first started. Some of the elements of the old education system have fallen by the wayside, but most of the subject matter is still with us. These things don't change because the marketable skills haven't changed much.

BS: Does this relate to the dilemma that the arts are valued less than the academic and technological skills?

MC: In most societies the artist can't compete with people with linguistic/ mathematical skills. I don't know of any society where the artist can compete in the marketplace. There might be one or two great artists who become mythical, superhuman figures. Even Michelangelo and Leonardo had to carve chests for the duke of Milan or whomever they were working for. They had to make practical things because there weren't extra resources to reward the artists. When you think of how much the carpenters and plumbers and managers of estates can do, you understand why they end up being on the top of the pyramid in material remuneration. The artist is more of a decoration. I don't see that changing too much in the future. I haven't seen it anywhere being very different. Even great musicians like Bach had to compose one cantata for each mass every week for the duke of Saxony or whomever.

The arts are fantastic and we have to make sure that people understand how important they are. But we—as a society—have to change first before we can have people take seriously how important the arts are. You have to actually change the way people value the arts. Otherwise you can't convince people that we have a choice between giving our children a good mathematics education or a musical one. It's no contest. Unfortunately, that's the reality. Once the values change to a certain extent, you can demonstrate that maybe the artist isn't going to make much money or have much power, but will have a happier life and be more satisfied with it. If you can show that, then maybe, slowly, people will take more seriously those means that allow you to reach that goal—of accepting the multiple intelligences in education.

BS: Wasn't part of Howard's goal in redefining intelligence to include creating and making things so that our essential understanding of intelligence includes artistic skills?

MC: Yes, I think that was a very good idea. His definition was an important part of why MI became so successful, because teachers value that. But sooner or later people tend to say, Yeah, sure, it's an intelligence, but it's a lower intelligence than the others because I just can't make any money with it.

People may not verbalize it this way but it must be in the subtext because that's why parents go along with today's simple-minded versions of what education is, which is embraced by our government and embodied in No Child Left Behind. Parents who realize that there is more to life than making a buck will say, Whoa, this approach to education is demeaning to our children. But most parents don't find anything wrong with the content of today's education. They think, Isn't that what children should learn?

There is still a lot of work to be done in education. We have to show that these other intelligences are valuable ways of relating to the world. That they have immediate rewards and are so enjoyable to children that in the long run it is going to make them happy and add up to a better life. If we can show them that, then people will slowly change.

Otherwise, people will just think that MI is an interesting and different way of thinking about intelligence but in terms of implications for education it won't go beyond the merely decorative. People need to feel that there's a payoff to being exposed to a different kind of education embodied in MI. There's a struggle in defining what that payoff is. Defining that payoff is more than what is measured by dollars and cents.

BS: Are you talking about educational experience that has intrinsic worth?

MC: I mean intrinsic in the sense that performance of the intelligence is in itself inherently rewarding. That's certainly true for some of the other intelligences, for example, kinesthetic, musical, and visual. I can claim that there is an intrinsic value to those, but whether or not those values generalize beyond the moment is another question. Because if it's just for the moment, then people can dismiss it by saying, "Yeah, it feels good to play basketball but it doesn't really add value to life otherwise."

BS: Isn't this where your work on intrinsic motivation complements MI? Because it's "enjoyment" that makes you a better person somehow. It's not merely "a pleasurable pasttime."

MC: Yes, eventually, this is where MI and intrinsic motivation should come together more.

BS: Intrinsic motivation emphasizes that what is important is the inner experience of being fulfilled by using your strengths to deal with challenges and to set achievable goals.

MC: Yes, of course, to me that is a very important idea. But I don't think you're going to have much success convincing many school districts that it should be part of schooling. Yes, there are schools here and there that are doing it, such as the Key Learning Community.

There is also the whole Danish educational system. Someone discovered a while ago that there is a clause in the Danish Constitution that says that children in the educational system should be taught to read, write, do sums, and *enjoy learning*. For 150 years this has been in the Danish Constitution but no one knew how to do that last thing. Then Hans Henrik Knoop in Denmark published articles on this in Danish educational journals. Now they officially recognize that MI is one way to think about how to promote an *enjoyment* for learning. There are schools and whole regions that have adopted MI and are given time to implement it.

It is one thing to prove that MI is a valid way to look at intelligence, but it is another to get people to realize that *the quality of experience* is what life is about. If you can enhance your quality of life by MI, it means that it is also growth producing, because you are learning something new by doing what you are best at doing. . . . Then you are improving life directly that way (and MI will gain acceptance).

So the future of MI might depend upon our ability to demonstrate that it adds value to a person's quality of life in the moment, as well as enhancing education for children so that they will become happier and more successful adults.

REFERENCE

Csikszentmihalyi, M. (1990). *Flow: The psychology of optimal experience*. New York: HarperPerennial.

FURTHER READING

Kunkel, C. (2007). The power of Key: Celebrating 20 years of innovation at the Key Learning Community, *Phi Delta Kappan, 89*(3), 204–209. Also available at www.616.ips.k12.in.us/

Knoop, H. H. (2008). *How the desire to learn may survive school*. Available at www .dpu.dk/site.aspx?p=11170&pureid=32693&puretype=pub&lang=eng&retur=1

CHAPTER 6

The Best of Both Worlds

Charles Murray

When I was evaluating social programs for disadvantaged youths during the 1970s, I was so certain that IQ tests were useless and even misleading that I did not bother to write down the IQ scores I found in my subjects' files. My first jolt came in 1982, when I read Arthur Jensen's *Bias in Mental Testing* (1980). In 1986, an invitation to comment on papers by Robert Gordon and Linda Gottfredson introduced me to social science's dark side of the moon: the extensive but ignored technical literature relating IQ scores to social and behavioral indicators of all sorts. I became a radical convert, a disciple of Charles Spearman and a believer in *g*, incensed at my colleagues who were unwilling to confront inconvenient data. I dismissed Howard Gardner's multiple intelligences (without actually reading what he had written) as politically correct claptrap.

Then, about the time Richard Herrnstein and I began work on *The Bell Curve*, I met Arthur Jensen. During the course of our conversation, Jensen observed that, in his opinion, Howard Gardner was the most original thinker writing about intelligence. Gardner was wrong on the psychometrics, of course, but that didn't make his insights less valuable. When I finally read Gardner, I understood. *Frames of Mind* (Gardner, 1983) was filled with fascinating observations about human abilities and opened up many new lines of inquiry. If Jensen, the preeminent expert on *g*, could make use of MI theory, why couldn't everybody? And why not look at *g* the same way? Thus the origin of my proposition: All of us will profit if we cheerfully render unto Spearman that which is Spearman's and render unto Gardner that which is Gardner's.

Taking this view doesn't mean that we can accept everything about both approaches. A theory of cognitive functioning based on MI and one based on *g* cannot both be completely right. In a decade or two, when we know pretty much the whole neuroscientific and genetic story of human abilities, one will have proved to be closer to the truth than the other. But as tools for thinking about the real world, MI and *g* are complementary, not antagonistic. Here are some large truths that I think congregants of both churches can accept:

> *People who write about human abilities should stop using the word "intelligence."* The word has acquired too much baggage, both positive and negative, and it has never been given an adequate scientific definition. Howard Gardner's solution is to label several abilities as intelligence, but, as he wrote in *Frames of Mind*, that choice is not essential: "I place no particular premium on the word *intelligence*. . . . If critics were willing to label language and logical thinking as talents as well, and to remove these from the pedestal they currently occupy, then I would be happy to speak of multiple talents" (Gardner, 1983, xi). Arthur Jensen is just as unhappy with *intelligence*, writing in *The g Factor* that "the term 'intelligence' should be discarded altogether in scientific psychology, just as it discarded 'animal magnetism' and as the science of chemistry discarded 'phlogiston'" (1998, 48). On this issue, there is no argument between Gardner and Jensen, nor need there be between their adherents. For myself, I will use the word *ability* rather than *intelligence* or *talent*.
>
> *When dealing with individuals, MI is the way to go.* I am thinking especially of children and their education. The unitary IQ score is self-evidently inferior to the separate measures of linguistic, logical-mathematical, and spatial abilities that can be extracted from IQ test batteries. If more precise tests of those abilities are available outside the IQ test framework, then we should use those tests instead. It is also self-evidently useful to have good measures of interpersonal and intrapersonal abilities. Measures of musical, bodily kinesthetic, and naturalistic ability are also useful, though less central to success in school. For that matter, there is no reason to limit ourselves to Gardner's inventory. Insofar as we have good measures of practical intelligence or emotional intelligence— I will let the experts sort out the claims that are being made for the existing measures—let us by all means throw them into the hopper as well. When dealing with individuals, the purpose of tests is appraisal and diagnosis. The more fine grained the portrait, the better. Whether the matrix of scores on those measures

shows a positive manifold is irrelevant, and so is the degree to which the individual measures load on the first factor. If a school system wants to administer an IQ test battery but never permit the full-scale IQ score even to be calculated, let alone circulated to teachers, it's fine with me.

When assessing the role of abilities in explaining macro social and economic phenomena, g *becomes useful.* Once again, theory is not the point; usefulness is the point. Three considerations lead me to continue to use the best available measure of *g*—IQ scores—when I am trying to understand how human abilities shape the world we live in.

The first consideration is that Gardner's eight abilities are self-evidently unequal in their relevance to adult life, and explorations of the relationship of various abilities to life's outcomes in large populations need to take that reality into account. Suppose we wish to examine the relationship that abilities have to (say) economic success, criminality, marital stability, and parenting practices.

Three of the abilities—bodily-kinesthetic, musical, and naturalistic—have a tiny relationship to earned income. Yo-Yo Ma and Kobe Bryant have high incomes largely as a result of their musical and bodily-kinesthetic ability, respectively, but they and their ilk are outliers lost in a shapeless cloud of dots signifying "no relationship" in samples of the general population. For criminality, marital stability, and parenting practices, it is hard to imagine any direct causal role that might be played by musical ability, bodily-kinesthetic, or naturalistic ability.

Spatial ability plausibly has wider relevance to occupations and thereby to earned income. If the dependent variable of interest were the ability to survive in a hunter-gatherer society, spatial ability would be exceptionally important. Being able to throw a spear accurately from point A to point B calls on spatial ability, and that skill confers a lot of reproductive fitness in such societies. So does the ability to find one's way home again after a long hunt. Spatial ability also has contemporary occupational value for engineers, architects, mathematics-intensive occupations, and crafts calling for fine hand-eye coordination. But I cannot think of any direct causal relationship that spatial ability might have to criminality, marital stability, or parenting practices.

This is not the case for good measures of interpersonal and intrapersonal ability. If earned income is the dependent variable, a general causal role is easy to imagine. It makes sense that high interpersonal ability in the form of charm or skill in reading others' motives will be related to economic success in life. It makes even more sense that high intrapersonal ability in characteristics such as self-discipline, industriousness, and persistence will have an independent role in explaining economic success. The same logic applies to criminality, marital stability, and parenting practices. In each case, the potential causal relevance is clear. Whether we already have good measures is beside the point. Good measures of interpersonal ability and intrapersonal ability would surely be useful.

The causal roles of linguistic ability and logical-mathematical ability are the most general and the most obvious of all. These abilities are all-purpose tools, with both direct and indirect causal relationships to all four dependent variables in my example. Regarding income, the known correlations between these abilities and measures of job productivity extend throughout the occupational ladder. It's not surprising. As every reader who ever worked as a waitress or busboy knows, such jobs can be done well or badly, efficiently or inefficiently, and the ways they are done well and efficiently call on skills such as memory, prioritizing, and (at least for the waitress) verbal facility. Linguistic ability and logical-mathematical ability also have pervasive indirect causal roles because of their effect on interpersonal and intrapersonal ability. One component of charm is verbal facility—a silver tongue—which is an aspect of linguistic ability. Part of the ability to read others' motives involves inference and deduction, both of which draw on logical-mathematical ability. Self-discipline, persistence, and industriousness are easier for people who can foresee and appropriately weigh long-term consequences and harder for people who cannot, and those tasks are easier or harder depending on logical-mathematical ability.

This brings me to the second reason why I continue to use IQ scores: We have quite good measures of the two all-purpose tools—linguistic ability and logical-mathematical ability—and quite good measures of spatial abilities involving the mental visualization and manipulation of objects. It is not necessary to have a certain opinion about factor analysis or about the validity of g as a construct to accept that point. No matter how "quite good" is assessed—predictive validity, face validity, or statistical reliability—the subtests of the major IQ batteries have a strong case to make for themselves that does not depend on Spearman's g. They are not perfect, but, compared with every other measure of every other complex construct in psychology, they are damn good.

And now the third consideration: If you are engaged in analyzing outcomes for large numbers of people, there is seldom any point in separating the measures of linguistic ability, logical-mathematical ability, and the ability to visualize and manipulate objects mentally. Exceptions exist. If you are exploring sex differences in mental processing, for example, there are reasons to keep the measures separate. But for outcomes such as economic success, criminality, marital stability, and parenting practices, disaggregating the measures seldom buys you anything. And if it is an empirical fact that, factor analyzed, the separate measures correlate with the first factor at around +.7 to +.9, there is a lot to be said for combining them. For most topics you lose nothing in terms of your ability to interpret the relationship of your separate measures to your dependent variables, and you gain something in the reliability and predictiveness of your combined measure.

A combined measure of linguistic ability, logical-mathematical ability, and the ability to visualize and manipulate objects mentally amounts to an IQ score. You do not need to call it *IQ*. In a book I just completed, I called it *academic ability*. Call it anything you want. Just accept that the IQ score is, in effect, a technically powerful measure of two and a half of Gardner's multiple intelligences and, more specifically, of the two and a half abilities that are both logically and empirically the most powerful predictors of outcomes in life among large groups.

It is possible to live comfortably with both MI and *g*. Indeed, to try to do otherwise limits us. To recognize the existence of many distinct human abilities is realistic. To insist that none of these abilities confers more human dignity on a person than any of the others is morally appropriate. To assess each child's strengths and weaknesses in all these abilities is essential. To pretend that they are equally important in the contemporary world is silly.

REFERENCES

Gardner, H. (1983). *Frames of mind: The theory of multiple intelligences* (1985 ed.). New York: Basic Books.
Jensen, A. R. (1980). *Bias in mental testing*. New York: Free Press.

FURTHER READING

Jensen, A. R. (1998). *The g factor: The science of mental ability*. Westport, CT: Praeger.
Murray, C. (1994). *The bell curve: Intelligence and class structure in American life*. New York: The Free Press.

Howard Gardner and the Use of Words

James R. Flynn

> *Maradona was a soccer genius.*
> *—Anyone who watched him play*

In 1983, Howard Gardner set a prerequisite and eight criteria for calling something an intelligence:

Prerequisite. A set of skills that solve problems and progress from the elementary to the advanced. The skills are not a set list. Those who have them often create new performances and discover new problems hitherto unknown. The skills must be socially valued.

Criterion 1. Autonomy on the physiological level; that is, it has its own locus in the brain so that trauma to that area can destroy or spare it.

Criterion 2. Autonomy on the psychological level; that is, we find individuals who excel in one area of competence even though they do not in others.

Criterion 3. It is triggered by a specific input, that is, by certain kinds of internally or externally presented information.

Criterion 4. It should have a developmental history, that is, matures by stages.

Criterion 5. It should have evolutionary antecedents.

Criterion 6. Its autonomy is confirmed by tasks that differentiate it from other intelligences.

Criterion 7. Its autonomy is confirmed by measurement; that is, instruments that rank people for its distinctive tasks indicate that it does not correlate (to a significant degree) with other measured intelligences.

Criterion 8. It is susceptible to being expressed in a symbolic system.

Applying these criteria, Gardner (1983) derived seven intelligences:

1. *Linguistic.* Mastery of the meaning of words and the syntax of language, with an ear for sound and an eye for imagery important for those few who become stylists or go on to write literature or poetry. Both they and rhetoricians must be aware of how language affects emotions.
2. *Logical-mathematical.* He emphasizes Piaget's developmental theories and that mathematics involves more than logic, such as the capacity to entertain long chains of logical relations expressed in symbolic form.
3. *Musical.* Performing music, which in a small number of cases leads on to musical composition, although composing can begin at an early age.
4. *Spatial.* Spatial visualization, seeing the continuity of a shape being rotated in space, and the power to create a mental image, which when highly developed is useful in mathematics and chess.
5. *Bodily-kinesthetic.* All areas in which control of the body or exploitation of its potential are central, such as sport, dance, mime, acting.
6. *Self-oriented personal intelligence.* A sense of personhood; self-knowledge of one's own feeling, capacities, and limitations; and control over one's behavior.
7. *Other-directed personal intelligence.* Knowing others in a way analogous to a mature knowledge of self, culminating in the kind of empathy that characterizes good teachers and therapists and great leaders. Note that these personal intelligences are not equivalent to mere sociability but rather, are forms of people-knowledge.

Ten years later Gardner (1993, p. xviii) said that he thought some form of spiritual intelligence might well exist, but for now he would stick to the original seven. Another 6 years later he rejected the claims of spiritual intelligence because of the lack of clarity of its content (1999, pp. 53–66). He felt more comfortable with existential intelligence and defined it as focused on ultimate issues: the significance of life, the meaning of death, the fate of the universe and the self, and profound experiences such as love or immersion in a work of art. (Kant called these experiences of the sublime.) He ends by concluding that even existential intelligence gets a quasi-pass at best. His prose is not entirely clear but he seems undecided about whether these experiences are mere emotions or whether, as Proust thought, they betokened some kind of reality.

He rejected a moral intelligence on the grounds that morality refers to the kind of person you are, that is, refers less to how you conceptualize morality and more to your character (1999, pp. 67–77). However, he did accept a new and eighth kind of intelligence called naturalistic intelligence. This refers to those expert in discerning the flora and fauna of their environment and those who go beyond nature to recognize automobiles by their sounds, discern artistic styles, and see novel patterns in the laboratory (pp. 48–52). Finally, he clarified kinesthetic intelligence by saying that it is the very bodily skill of the athlete or dancer or surgeon that earns the accolade. He stresses the enormous amount of practice and expertise that goes into their performances and believes that they suffer from snobbish attitudes that reflect the Cartesian distinction between mind and body (pp. 95–96).

In labeling his eight constructs, Gardner is mainly concerned that they all be called the same name, no matter whether it is "intelligences" or "talents." This is because he believes that the two terms constitute a value hierarchy. Therefore, calling what IQ tests measure (linguistic and logical-mathematical competence) intelligence and calling excellence at dance a talent devalues dancing. It implies that those who lack the IQ skills but have outstanding kinesthetic or musical abilities are not smart but dumb (Gardner, 1983, p. xi; 1993, p. xx).

I will discuss two issues, one of values and one of language, although the two are intertwined. First, I accept that there is a value hierarchy implied here. But implying that things are of equal value is no more or less a value judgment than ranking them. Urging that we accept his evaluation puts Gardner just as much in the position of an advocate as those who rank competences. There is nothing wrong with advocating a change in how most people evaluate things but we should give our reasons. As far as I can see, Gardner's reasoning runs as follows: (1) We all know that it is arbitrary to single out some socially valued competences as more valuable than others; (2) the present use of the word "intelligence" does exactly that; (3) therefore, we should either drop the word or alter its usage to keep it from doing mischief.

Second, do we really want to stop saying that people who are good at something like dance are "dumb"? None of us wants to be insulting but it may make perfect sense to use some term that singles out for emphasis that they are "cognitively" below average or even cognitively unable to cope with everyday life. In other words, the value question does not settle the usage question. Even if we wish that everyone would value all humane competences the same, we may feel that eliminating the use of the word "intelligence" will be counterproductive.

I should make it clear that I stopped reading Gardner in 1993 with the sole exception of his 1999 book (*Intelligence Reframed*). I did not need to be convinced that there are a variety of significant human competences and that seemed to be the important point of his theory. Therefore, what follows is circumscribed. But it rehearses why I stopped reading and offers others a chance to say why I was mistaken. I should add that my neglect had nothing to do with whether his followers were doing good studies of various human competences or developing good instruments for counseling. It was simply a matter that these were not my core interests.

THE RICHNESS OF ORDINARY LANGUAGE

As for common usage, Gardner (1993, p. x) urges us to try to forget that we have ever heard of the concept of intelligence as a single property of the human mind. Ordinary language already does that in the sense that we all know of people who use words intelligently but who are hopeless at mathematics. Nonetheless, in ordinary language, one use of the word "intelligence" is preeminent, namely, using it to refer to cognitive intelligence. What is meant by "cognitive" is that this kind of intelligence involves holding in mind a wide range of meanings or concepts or relationships, often a highly complex web, either near simultaneously or in succession. This usage has an enviable lineage.

Just as the human brain has evolved, words have evolved. In its cognitive sense, quickness and completeness of mental apprehension, the word "intelligence" came into use in English in the 16th century and was well established by the time Burke used it in 1780. However, it was a loan word from Latin and had a predecessor, still used today, the word "wit," which meant the same thing. "Wit" is found as far back as *Beowulf* in 589. It derives from even older words in Proto-Germanic and Proto-Indo-European but at that time, it had not yet been sharpened to mean cognitive intelligence. Its remote ancestor meant simply to perceive or find. Nonetheless, a word that has been around for almost 1,500 years probably has a job to do. Its job was to let Beowulf say things like "He may not have much wit, but he a great warrior and inspires his men in battle by his example."

This does not prevent ordinary language from making distinctions that clarify the abilities of those who are good at music or sport. For example, in regard to cricket, we can distinguish two kinds of excellences, cognitive excellence and wonderful skills. New Zealand's Jeremy Coney was often called an intelligent cricketer, meaning that he had mastered the cognitive problems of cricket. He knew how to place his men in the slips, calculate the odds for and against bringing the outfield closer in, and when to switch bowlers. He was a master of the strategy of the game and that is why he was made captain. There were others whose trained bodies could play the game better. They were better batters and fielders; that is, they had better "kinesthetic skills," if you will. But they were not made captain. They were not intelligent enough.

Now, it can be argued that even wonderful skills have something akin to a cognitive component. Ordinary language recognizes this when it calls Maradona a "soccer genius." He had no capacity for cognitive complexity in most settings but he had something more than wonderful ball skills. When he had the ball, he seems to have had a complete awareness of the positions of his own team and his opponents and, above all, the goalie. No one would have called him a genius without his ball skills but he did have something extra. Larry Bird had the same apparent comprehensive "map" of where players were on the basketball court.

I do not mean to imply that the cognitive complexity a genius exhibits exists only on the conscious level. Maradona and Bird reacted in a split second, and their "maps" must have been almost subliminal. The cognitive complexity of the concepts Newton's mind had to encompass to create the new physics had to be present in his mind even when he was not cogitating about them. I know very well how far I fall short of genius. But even I find that I suddenly have an eureka moment right after I get out of bed because my mind had been turning over problems in my sleep. Even a good extemporaneous lecturer must have many concepts present in working memory when speaking on a difficult topic.

So there is a cognitive component in sporting excellence that goes beyond what is conveyed by the phrase "a well-trained body" and ordinary language uses "genius" to recognize this. As to why it withholds the word "intelligence," I suspect it is because of the cognitive complexity gap between what Newton held in mind and what even the greatest sportsman does. But my point is this. Ordinary language at present can name the similarity between Maradona and Newton insofar as it exists. It does not need the vocabulary of multiple intelligences to do the job.

In music, we use the word "genius" even more freely because it may be that there is no cognitive complexity gap between Newton and Mozart. Some say that Mozart could hold in mind simultaneously the entire structure of a symphony, with all the orchestration of the various instruments and the progression of its four movements somehow all of a piece (it is not clear that Mozart himself made such a claim). This is such an impressive cognitive complexity that if all Gardner wanted was to popularize the term "musical intelligence," I doubt that most people would object. But once again, do we really need it to give the proper accolade? It may be said that the word "genius" goes only to those who were the best in the world and that someone like Offenbach deserves a measure of praise. Well, we can say that he had a wonderful inventiveness for melody and brilliant orchestral colors. Certainly this describes the debt we owe him better than saying that while not the equal of Mozart, he was well above average in musical intelligence.

In addition, reserving the word *intelligence* for cognitive intelligence is very efficient. In every field, we want to distinguish between those who have it and those who do not. Not just to distinguish between Coney and Maradona, but also between a great boxer and the second in his corner who plots strategy in the ring, and between someone who can cognize about music (a critic) and someone who cannot but is an accomplished performer. Some performers are great critics as well but they need not be. Perhaps the most tedious interviews ever recorded have been those with jazz musicians talking about their art ("it all comes down to how yuh blows it").

There are great literary scholars and critics who do not have the talent to write a novel. There are people who are tedious when they talk about political ideas but who have keen people-knowledge. *Mein Kampf* is painful to read but who could match Hitler's knowledge of the frustrations of the German masses? The latter involved much less cognitive complexity than the former but it made him into an extraordinary politician. In sum, I see no conceptual clarity to be gained by revising ordinary usage. I pass on to the question of values.

WORDS AND THEIR ASSOCIATED VALUES

Words have associations that often encapsulate values and we may want to challenge the value hierarchy that is dominant. Before we do, we should answer some questions: Why do most people adhere to the present hierarchy? Why, if at all, do we want to challenge it? and What is the best way of doing so? We should also specify what cap we are wearing: that of a parent or child or that of a humanist and advocate.

Parents and Children

Most people, of course, are merely parents or children operating in American society or some other developed society or some society that hopes to develop. In these settings, cognitive intelligence naturally acquires associations that do not transfer readily to things like musical and athletic ability. Indeed, cognitive intelligence has wide-ranging and intense positive associations that render it unique. The most obvious sign of this is that it is valued at a level far less exacting than athletic or musical or creative skills. As society has become more integrated in the modern era, you have to be so very good as a basketball player, or a pianist, or a composer to make your way.

Parents feel uneasy if they see their children pinning all their hopes on a sport, or the violin, or singing because they know that only a few can make these things more than a hobby. And if the same child lacks cognitive intelligence, they really begin to worry. Cognitive intelligence, all the way down to below the mean, if used, opens so many doors, and if it is lacking society may not find a valued place for their child. To hear someone say of your child, "He is not very bright but watch how he hits the ball," and know that it is true, is not pleasant. You know that to play pro baseball, he will have to be in the top 1/1000th of 1%. Falling short of that, and being below average in cognitive intelligence, he will not even be able to be a sports reporter. In other words, you know how much more socially valued cognitive intelligence is, how much more useful it is, and these create the associations that make you feel sick at hearing your child denied it.

The brute fact is that cognitive intelligence carries positive associations at modest levels that the other forms of "intelligence" match only at the highest level. And these associations are so matched to cognitive intelligence that it seems peculiar to label other things as intelligences that lack its essence. The word "holy" is a label for a reverential and obedient relationship to God. You could call a great musician "holy" became of his reverential and obedient relationship to his art, despite the fact that he is an atheist and a womanizer. But it has positive associations with its religious setting that inhibit its use in secular settings.

Gardner says that some have castigated the usage he wishes to introduce because it expands the capacity of the word "intelligence" to label people negatively. After all, most people of below-average IQ have no outstanding talent in music or sport and many are not particularly good at people-knowledge. It is bad enough to be told you are dumb once without being told you are dumb in eight different ways.

At least one kind of multiple intelligence assessment has eight main scales broken down into 26 descriptive subscales. This increases the possibility of a good score somewhere. However, unless you are dealing with someone who is not very acute, it would be daunting to know that you are poor on 20 scales and mediocre on 4, particularly if the 4 seem pretty trivial.

Gardner says that those who use multiple intelligences to label negatively are importing the "abuses" of IQ testing into multiple intelligence theory, and he is hardly to blame for that. He states that he does not believe that "it is possible to assess intelligences in pure form" and that the assessments he advocates differ from IQ assessments (Gardner, 1993, p. xxii).

The talk of not being able to measure pure intelligence is irrelevant. When a child on the playground is humiliated by being called dumb, his playmates are not judging his pure intelligence or intrinsic potential. They are saying that he is operationally dumb, that he behaves unintelligently, without any assessment of the relative contributions of genes and environment.

As for summing up the test results, why is it an "abuse" to say that someone is low on skill after skill? Here we must distinguish four things: whether a measure would in principle allow you to rank people; whether you design the measure to specify a ranking, or only to determine whether someone can do various tasks; what information it is helpful to tell the person assessed; and how you should do it.

Gardner concedes that his measures could in principle rank people because, if that is not possible, a competency cannot qualify as an intelligence. His Criterion 2 says that there must be individuals who excel in one area of competence even though they do not in others. Criterion 7 demands that how one kind of intelligence ranks people does not correlate (to a significant degree) with how another kind does.

You can, of course, use a battery that gives no estimate of ranking simply by failing to gather the required information. You can forego selecting a representative sample to norm the test. Without such you cannot say at what percentile of the general population anyone lies even on one of the 26 subscales. So now you use the subscales only to determine whether someone can do A (can discern pitch) or B (can learn to read music) or C (has manual dexterity). And as to what you tell the subject, you can certainly use tact, that is, withhold bad news and put a positive spin on the results. Never use the word "deficient" and always talk about "strengths" even if they are few and feeble. There is nothing to be censured in this, in that everyone does it. IQ tests are often disguised as some other kind of test and neither the child nor the parent is given the score. The reason the SAT is so filled with angst is that the scores are the whole point and have to be made explicit.

Filtering information to avoid comparisons with others is fine when you are trying to find out how children might best spend their time at school. But sooner or later, you must give career counseling. Then the chips are down and at least rough rankings have to be made explicit, if only out of sheer humanity. "Sally, you have been a good basketball player here at university but you are not going to make it in the WBA; what about coaching?" "Johnny, you have practiced your piano as much as I could ask but you will not get into Julliard; you have done well in pre-law, why not go to law school and enjoy your music on the side?" A Gardner assessment may be less wounding than others because those who administer the scales are encouraged to show more tact. However, tact has its limits. Whatever record of performance is made the basis of counseling, no amount of tact can soften advice about giving up career aspirations that are deeply held.

If tact is an objective, it cannot be helpful to call the measures "multiple intelligence scales" rather than "multiple ability scales." I would have thought it best to get as far away from the word "intelligence" as possible and call them "developmental guidance scales."

Humanists and Advocates

Parents and children tacitly accept that cognitive intelligence has more social significance than other kinds of talents. This hierarchy reflects social reality and it would be dishonest to tell them the contrary. But we are not just participants in society; we judge it and sometimes find it wanting. Let us put on the new cap of someone who holds humanist ideals. When I do that, I conclude that the market gives activities that others value (and are willing to pay for) supremacy over the things many of us would want to do to live as rich a life as possible.

I argue here that there are innumerable valuable traits, such as self-knowledge, empathy, sympathy, social awareness, self-control, courage, love of the good, critical acumen, wisdom, and artistic and physical prowess, that are as important or more important than intelligence. As a keen sportsman, I particularly dislike those who discount athletic excellence. (However, I do not wish to prejudice anyone against Descartes' views on dualism by naming him as a culprit.) In my book *The Hollow Center* (2008) I go even further. I try to convince the reader that Athens was a better society than Carthage, and suggest a Social Democratic program that would mitigate the consequences of the market by allowing people to pursue excellences that have little cash value.

I suspect that Gardner shares my humane-egalitarian moral ideals (I know nothing of his politics). But there is no short cut toward getting people to evaluate one another differently. Uniformity of labels for various competencies will affect only the already converted. And in 1983, one group existed that was already converted. Gardner did not anticipate that educationists would find his theory so congenial (1993, p. ix). I would have. Educationists whose hearts overrule their heads discredit egalitarianism by trying to create a world in which no one is ranked above anyone else— the sort of teacher who wants to do away with grades, or with keeping score when two teams compete during sports time.

They see Gardner as a vehicle for praising every child as good at something. I am certain that he does not share their naïveté. But a few words on why giving all human competencies nondiscriminatory labels is futile. Positive associations cluster around words precisely because they evolve in a certain social setting. The links between the word and its associations and its traditional setting becomes so powerful that they are not easily broken.

In the case of cognitive intelligence, it is impossible to transfer its associations to a new usage in a new setting. A teacher may call a basketball player who is cognitively backward "kinesthetically intelligent" but the powerful positive associations of cognitive intelligence will not transfer. His mates know that he is just good at basketball. No use of the word "intelligence" will surround him with the aura of someone whose kind of intelligence puts the world at his feet; and gives him his pick of company from among those who want to be around someone whose conversation is intelligent and interesting. A test of kinesthetic intelligence may label a child "dumb" but neither children nor their parents will react as they would to an assessment of cognitive deficiency. They will merely say, "All right, Susie is not very good at ballet or netball," something they probably knew already from watching her perform.

The reason the associations will not transfer is that the words in question refer to assessments that are within the competence of most people, made day in and day out about observed behavior, and conjure up no threat to the body politic. Cases in which transferring words do transfer associations are quite different.

Take the word "fascist." Political judgments are subtle, are made mainly in times of strong emotion, are often about intentions alone, and can conjure up nightmarish threats. The word "fascist" accumulated a huge negative aura because of Hitler's crimes and the danger he posed. Inevitably, everyone started calling people fascists who were one step to the right of them on the political spectrum. Humane, racially unbiased, social democrats become "Social Fascists" simply because they do not advocate revolutionary tactics (which were supposed to be necessary to depose "fascists" like British prime ministers and U.S. presidents). However, once the external threat disappeared, the word lost its bite because everyone was using it as a devalued word. It now meant only "anyone I consider less radical than I am." Calling someone a "Communist" who is a step to the left of you had a longer shelf life because the USSR was around a lot longer than Hitler's Germany. But in the postwar era, soft on Communism has given way to soft on terrorism.

Those who consider men a "foreign enemy" tried to transfer the horror that surrounds the word "rape." That word, in its original setting, deserved all the opprobrium it had as naming a violent, exploitive, and destructive act. However, calling it rape if a wife slept with her husband to please him when she was not in the mood did not work very well. Accusing a logging company of rape when it cut down a tree is doing better. Still, it sometimes sobers manipulators of language who can think when their usage comes back to bite them. Recently, a New Zealand gang leader was asked about the fact that some of the gang members had perpetrated rape. He countered with "What kind of rape are we talking about, environment rape, married rape, or what?" He had learned to play the game.

I think it is counterproductive to try to confer prestige on a variety of human traits by calling them all intelligences. The implication is that intelligence is so preeminently valuable that for anything else to rival it, it must be called an intelligence. If the common task of humanists is to persuade people that other things are equally or more valuable than intelligence, how can we do that when the very vehicle we use implies the contrary? We have sold the pass.

THE VIEW FROM THE TOWER

My critique may seem tied to the perspective of upwardly mobile Western society, but it is not. To illuminate its multicultural validity, I return to Gardner's concern about the fact that our society uses the word "intelligence" to label various human excellences in a way that implies a value hierarchy. It is true that Americans tend to accept a hierarchy that puts linguistic and logical-mathematical skills at the top, perhaps personal skills next, perhaps musical and kinesthetic skills next, with naturalistic skills near the bottom.

However, every living, breathing culture has a hierarchy; they just have different ones. Medieval society would put the half-rejected existentialist intelligence at the top, perhaps the kinesthetic skill of the warrior-knight next, perhaps the monkish skills of language and mathematics next, and so forth. Australian aboriginal culture would put naturalistic skills (distinguishing the flora and fauna of the physical environment) at the very top, existential intelligence next, musical and kinesthetic (dance) next, and so forth. It would be quite incredible if we found an actual culture that just happened to put all eight of Gardner's intelligence on an equal footing. And every society will evolve a language that reflects its own peculiar hierarchy.

The only one who has a culture-free view is someone who stands at the top of an anthropological tower, looks down on all human societies, and judges them. But no one actually lives at the top of that tower. It is a perspective that is worthwhile because it allows us to transcend our cultural blinders and ask questions like, Have we gone too far in terms of a rigid hierarchy? Should we perhaps offer compensation to those whose skills are near the bottom? and Do we not want everyone to feel that he or she has a valued place in our society? Again, I would answer all those questions in the affirmative. That obliges me to try to change attitudes.

Now reflect: Does anyone think we could flatten the hierarchy rooted in Aboriginal culture by some kind of relabeling? So how much contribution will relabeling make in the United States? We really do have a culture. If you want to alter it, nothing can lighten the arduous task of analysis, persuasion, and forging a consensus in favor of a more humane and egalitarian society. Packing a prestigious word into your luggage and carrying it hither and thither will not deposit its prestige wherever you happen to stop.

OTHER MATTERS

I make no judgment about the clinical utility of the 26 scales that implement the assessment of multiple competencies. Perhaps they offer bad advice that an IQ test would avoid. For example, a child scores low on mathematical ability and above average on musical ability and is advised to focus on the latter. It may be that he or she has been bored by school math, and music is only a passing interest. A high IQ score would veto foreclosing the mathematical option. But for the sake of argument, assume that properly interpreted Gardner-type scales are without peer in offering developmental advice. Then everyone should use them. But that is a virtue separate from language; that is, it owes absolutely nothing to what the scales are called.

It is possible that Gardner's intense interest in a variety of desirable human skills brought a better balance to research, for example, more emphasis on the brain physiology that underlies sporting skills, musical skills, empathic skills, and so forth. The sports physiologists I have spoken to were unaware of the theory of multiple intelligences. A lot of people have always been interested in the psychological and physiological roots of artistic creation. I leave this question to the historians. They might compare the breadth of research in the United States, where he is much read, with what exists in nations in which he is less read (England or the Communist bloc in its athletic heyday).

RELIGION AND WOODY ALLEN

Gardner's concepts do not improve on ordinary language and will not reprioritize or humanize how people assess one another. If we succeed in our advocacy of humane values and a more egalitarian society, the hierarchy implied in "intelligence" versus "talent" will have been drained of its venom. If we do not succeed, nothing will do the job for us. Digging your heels in on using nondiscriminatory terms for human competences just affirms the depth of your own commitment to egalitarian ideals. It does not alter the value judgments implicit in ordinary language, nor should it be sufficient to do so. As for ranking people in terms of various competences, that is only honest. It is not a threat akin to Hitler or Stalin.

I am glad that Gardner held the line on religious intelligence. He is correct that nothing seems too absurd to be the object of veneration. I make an exception for the great mystics (not all of whom were religious) in that many years of study have convinced me that the mystical experience plays a role in human perfection. But I do not want to start talking about mystical intelligence or even genius. The core of the experience has nothing to do with cognitive complexity but rather involves unparalleled simplicity. We can distinguish intelligent mystics from unintelligent ones, but this is a matter of identifying those who demonstrate cognitive intelligence when they talk about their experience. Saint John of the Cross talks sense while Saint Teresa of Avilla gushes.

I hope that no one is tempted by existential intelligence. Concern about ultimate questions is a mixed bag. The ones that make sense to cogitate about, such as the status of our ethical ideals and human autonomy, are my major scholarly specialty. When I think about them, I am aware of no special talent kicking in that is different from thinking about the theory of intelligence. As for Gardner's other ultimate questions, life is what you make of it, death is when life stops, the beginning and end of the cosmos is best left to the physicists, and the sublime feelings I get from love and art are good enough for me. Fortunately, there are those with comic genius who keep us from getting too solemn. When Woody Allen was asked what he regretted most about life, he said: "The time I spent reading John Fowles's novel *The Magus*."

REFERENCES

Gardner, H. (1983). *Frames of mind*. New York: Basic Books.

Gardner, H. (1993). Introduction. In *Frames of mind: Tenth-anniversary edition*. New York: Basic Books.

Gardner, H. (1999). *Intelligence reframed*. New York: Basic Books.

FURTHER READING

Flynn, J. R. (2007). *What is intelligence? Beyond the Flynn effect*. Cambridge: Cambridge University Press

Flynn, J. R. (2008). *The hollow center: Race, class, and ideas in America*. Cambridge: Cambridge University Press.

Jensen, A. R. (1998). The *g* factor and the design of education. In R. J. Sternberg & W. M. Williams (Eds.), *Intelligence, instruction, and assessment: Theory into practice* (pp. 111–131). Mahwah, NJ: Lawrence Erlbaum.

CHAPTER 8

Multiple Intelligences in Practice

Linda Darling-Hammond

The great African American cleric Howard Thurman was fond of telling a story that I recount here with minor amendments:

> Once in the Animal Kingdom, there was a decree from the new Overseer of Education—that each animal would need to achieve mastery in a set of basic skills essential to animal life. These skills were flying, hopping, running, and swimming. Now the Kingdom had some magnificent animals. The eagle could fly further and faster than any bird in any other nation on the continent. The kangaroo could hop higher and farther than any other marsupial anywhere. The gazelle could run more swiftly and gracefully than any land animal from here to the setting sun. And the porpoise could swim and jump and dive more beautifully than anything else in the Sea. These abilities allowed them to protect the Kingdom from every vantage point, and the Kingdom was a safe and prosperous place as a result.
>
> The animals had spent a great deal of time perfecting their talents, but had rarely tried to master one anothers' skills. But they were willing to try. They worked and worked at it with all their might. The eagle learned to hop passably, but had a devil of a time running and nearly drowned trying to swim. In fact he damaged his feathers so badly, he could no longer fly very far. The Kangaroo took to running. But swimming taxed her tiny arms dreadfully and her attempts to fly by throwing herself from the top of a tall ledge

caused her to break a leg, so she could no longer hop. The gazelle met the same fate in the flying lesson, and the two of them now limped around pitifully together. The porpoise developed his own form of flying and hopping in the water—though this was frowned on by the schoolmaster as highly unorthodox—but simply could not figure out how to run, and finally became so dehydrated squirming about on the land, that he had to be hospitalized. At this point, with no one to patrol the skies or the sea, and no scouts on the land, the Animal Kingdom was invaded by a hostile force and taken over for a period of time, until the animals recovered enough of their abilities to recapture their land. In the effort to mimic one another, they had nearly lost themselves and their magnificent abilities— each special and each essential to the functioning of the Kingdom as a whole.

This story, which is a story about the value of diverse abilities and the dangers of standardization, is also in many ways a tale of multiple intelligences. It conveys the importance of appreciating and developing the distinctive highly developed abilities that individuals possess.

Howard Gardner (1993) made a similar point in *Multiple Intelligences: The Theory in Practice*, when he defined intelligence as the ability to solve problems or fashion products that are valued in the full realm of human activity:

> Think, for example, of sailors in the South Seas, who find their way around hundreds, or even thousands of islands by looking at the constellations of stars in the sky, feeling the way a boat passes over the water, and noticing a few scattered landmarks. A word for intelligence in a society of these sailors would probably refer to that kind of navigational ability. Think of surgeons and engineers, hunters and fishermen, dancers and choreographers, athletes and athletic coaches, tribal chiefs and sorcerers. All of these different roles need to be taken into account if we accept the way I define intelligence—that is, as the ability to solve problems, or to fashion products, that are valued in one or more cultural or community settings. (p. 3)

Gardner has noted that exclusive reliance in education on the usually favored verbal and logical intelligences would produce a nation full of law professors, something that no society could manage, much less desire. And while teachers have to a large extent embraced the notion that cultivating individual talent is an important role of schools, the standardizing influences of policy generally have not. I am often reminded of this fable when I see the results of exit exam testing in states where students must pass exams in four or five different subject areas in order to graduate, and young people who are highly skilled in some areas but struggle in another see their hopes for a productive life squelched even before it begins. This is quite often the case with exceptional-needs students who excel in particular areas despite their challenges in others, and with recent immigrants who, for example, are highly adept in mathematics although they struggle with the English language or do not have a base of knowledge in U.S. history. In an effort to create standardized outcomes, schools often feel compelled to adopt standardized methods, making it even more difficult for students to use the ways they learn most effectively to help them develop new abilities, or to develop the abilities they have.

Multiple intelligence (MI) theory is grounded both in an appreciation for human diversity and in a recognition that many abilities are worth developing, within and across individuals, in addition to those required for basic reading, writing, and mathematics. In fact, these other intelligences—spatial, musical, interpersonal, intrapersonal, and bodily-kinesthetic—can often create useful pathways into developing essential literacy and quantitative skills, as well as playing valuable roles in their own right. I think if this understanding had been widespread 25 years ago, when Gardner first published *Frames of Mind,* we might have had a different outcome from another major report issued in 1983—*A Nation at Risk,* which led to many of the standardizing influences that Gardner's work warns against.

Still, multiple intelligences theory has had an important influence on teaching and on teacher education, and it has changed life and learning for students and teachers in many schools. In what follows, I will talk about both conceptual and practical breakthroughs that have occurred in the field and what these have meant for life in classrooms.

CONCEPTUAL BREAKTHROUGHS

Over the 20th century, American schools were much influenced by the view of intelligence as a unidimensional, fixed, innate capacity—something one is born with in a given quantity that is revealed on an IQ test. This view has led to early sorting and tracking in schools, allocating different curriculum opportunities to different students and limiting expectations in ways that reduce effort and growth. Whereas some other countries, particularly Asian nations, start with assumptions that every student can learn with effort and good teaching, the U.S. tradition has been to assume that differences in performance are predetermined and should guide placements in curriculum tracks, streams, or lanes that determine learning opportunities. A side effect of this ability-based view is that it has too often persuaded both students and teachers that effort-based strategies should not be a primary focus of how schoolwork is organized. Practices like cooperative learning and revising work to meet standards have often been viewed as "cheating," because they focus more on ultimate success than on initial individual ability.

By contrast, Gardner's work suggests that teachers have an opportunity and an obligation to teach in a variety of ways that enable students to connect to the material and to learn. Furthermore, Gardner notes that intelligence is developed in cultural contexts; and it is not merely about abstractions but encompasses problem solving and performance, including the production of products, not just the answering of artificially constructed questions on standardized tests. And many teachers and teacher education programs have taken this view to heart, working today on very different presumptions about what the teacher's job is.

According to Gardner, an effective education builds a bridge between the content being taught and the students in the classroom:

> On the one hand, educators need to recognize the difficulties students face in attaining genuine understanding of important topics and concepts. On the other hand, educators need to take into account the differences among minds and, as far as possible, fashion an education that can reach the infinite variety of students. (Gardner 1999, p. 186)

This view is similar to the conception of the task of 21st-century education articulated by Bob Glaser (1990): that schools must move from a selective mode, "characterized by minimal variation in the conditions for learning" in which "a narrow range of instructional options and a limited number of paths to success are available" (p. 16), to an adaptive mode in which "conceptions of learning and modes of teaching are adjusted to individuals—their backgrounds, talents, interests, and the nature of their past performances and experiences" (p. 17).

This creates a radically different conceptualization of the purposes and strategies for education from that represented by the 20th-century quest for a "one best system" (Tyack, 1974) that standardizes every aspect of the teaching and learning process. This new framework has led to new approaches to conceptualizing teaching and learning. These approaches, prominent in reforms of teacher education, as well as curriculum and assessments in some states during the 1990s, have the following features:

- Teachers see their role as learning to identify students' strengths, providing entry points and pathways into subject matter, enabling connections, and encouraging students to represent their understanding in different ways.
- Educational goals and strategies are broadened beyond linguistic and logical-mathematical competences to include working with others, developing a sense of one's own abilities, creating, performing, and problem solving in different areas.

- Teachers look for varying ways for students to learn and demonstrate learning, as well as differing types of products. Having school assignments and assessments become more reflective of the real world of human activity is important for our development as human beings, as societies need many kinds of people with a range of abilities that are developed to high levels.

Although the mountain of assumptions is large, Gardner's work has also raised questions about the cultural neutrality of IQ tests and notions of intelligence, reinforcing other work that has pointed out that tests of this kind are embedded in culturally based referents that may underestimate the knowledge and abilities of children whose experiences are not part of the dominant culture. Such tests also privilege certain ways of knowing and modes of performance over others (e.g., National Research Council, 1982; Sternberg, 1997). The unquestioning acceptance of these measures has also been shaken, if not entirely dislodged, in schools as a function of this work.

PRACTICAL BREAKTHROUGHS:
MULTIPLE INTELLIGENCES IN THE CLASSROOM

Clearly, since the publication of *Frames of Mind*, MI theory has had a great impact on schools and teachers. Of course, as with all major theories, there have been many misunderstandings. For example, in some places, you can see efforts to find out which intelligences a person "has" and notions that if a student "has" an intelligence, he or she should always produce products in a particular modality. This has in some cases led to much cutting and pasting and doing of posters to reflect artistic intelligences, rather than writing of papers or development of more intellectually challenging products. Not every educator has understood that the art of teaching is helping people to use their already well-developed abilities to build other strengths, so that they can master important learning in a variety of ways.

These kinds of misunderstandings are inevitable with all big ideas that are widely disseminated. But there are indications of positive outcomes: For example, in a study of 41 schools using MI theory, researchers found that putting MI theory into practice was associated with improved test scores, improved student behavior, improved parent participation, and positive outcomes for students identified with learning disabilities (Kornhaber, Fierros, & Veenema, 2003). Interviews with principals and teachers in these schools suggested that using MI theory supported instruction in several ways: It provided teachers with a framework for discussing children's strengths and weaknesses; it promoted the arts, including music, drama, and dance; and it promoted individualization of education and choice in the classroom. Perhaps the most prominent ways teachers have drawn on Gardner's theory in their classrooms include these three:

- Assessing and building on students' strengths,
- Providing points of entry to subject matter, and
- Developing curricula and assessments that create connections among ideas and multiple approaches to demonstrating competence.

We have learned some things from practice in the field about how to use this important work to enable teachers to become more skilled and successful with a broader range of students. Below, I talk about some of this learning and implications for teaching and teacher education.[1]

ASSESSING AND BUILDING ON STUDENTS' STRENGTHS

Teachers who have learned to teach with an awareness of multiple intelligences and pathways can identify the areas where students excel and provide opportunities for students with different kinds of minds to flourish and to find pathways into all kinds of material. Teachers can be taught to identify individual differences through careful observation of activities that reveal strengths, preferences, and abilities (see, e.g., Darling-Hammond, 2006). Once these differences are identified, instruction can provide supports for students who learn in different ways.

A vivid example of the value of this kind of diagnostic assessment is provided in the account of Akeem, a third-grade student who entered Susan Gordon's classroom in a New York City elementary school after having been expelled for throwing a desk at a teacher in another school (Darling-Hammond, Ancess, & Falk, 1995, pp. 217–224). In the early weeks of school, Akeem had outbursts of temper, made frequent efforts to disrupt classroom meetings, and was either periodically surly or aggressive. Gordon immediately began a focused effort to assess Akeem's strengths as well as to locate where he found difficulty.

Along with completing a set of individualized assessments that helped her determine his progress in literacy and numeracy, she documented exactly when and under what circumstances his outbursts occurred. She also carefully documented those moments when Akeem seemed most at ease, focused, and productive. She discovered that Akeem's misbehavior tended to occur when certain kinds of academic tasks arose: his actions seemed designed to deflect attention from the fact that he could not read well or write with any ease. At the same time, she discovered that he was very interested and skilled at complex and creative drawings, and he displayed a passion for and strength in building and designing architectural models.

Susan encouraged Akeem to work in hands-on learning centers that tapped his artistic skills and his abilities to construct machines and models. Because her close assessments of his reading and writing had identified particular areas where he struggled, she was able to develop a plan that would help provide him some focused instruction with those needs in mind. She found him books and developed writing assignments that built on his interests, while systematically teaching him new strategies for reading.

Gradually in concert with these activities and assessments, Akeem began to experience greater success academically. Akeem developed architectural drawings and drew sophisticated graphic images, which he later annotated and turned into comic books. As he was recognized by peers for his artistic and spatial abilities and began to gain status in the classroom, he joined classroom activities with increasing enthusiasm. Not incidentally, he learned to read and write. Akeem was able to finish middle school with a solid academic record and near perfect attendance and gained admission into a specialized high school for the arts.

Akeem's story provides an illustration of how to diagnose learning strengths and needs and how to build a set of teaching strategies that addresses these needs by using productive pathways into understanding. These possibilities are available in classrooms on a daily basis. For instance, students who are interested in art can be given the choice of first illustrating an idea or topic and then composing a story; students who seem particularly strong in spatial thinking can be given the opportunity to work with manipulatives to explore mathematical concepts; students who exhibit strong interpersonal skills can be called on to lead a group investigation. This approach leads to stronger engagement, fewer classroom management problems, and deeper learning—as well as development of an academic identity that current research has demonstrated is a critically important variable in maintaining effort and doing the hard work needed to develop greater competence.

Akeem's example also illustrates another point, about how teachers construct motivation and engagement. In contrast to the common view, motivation is not wholly intrinsic to the student, nor is it just about interest or "excitement." Motivation is developed when learners encounter engaging tasks at which they believe they can and will succeed because the teacher offers the entryway and supports for them to develop competence. For students to remain motivated in school, they need opportunities to succeed in learning.

Observation plays an important role in understanding students' profiles of learning and development. Krechevsky and Seidel (1998) suggest that teachers look for the following things so they may develop better understandings of individual students:

- What choices do students make when given options?
- What roles do they play when working together?
- How do they handle unanticipated problems?
- What captures their attention? When do they lose interest?
- What problem-solving strategies do they offer?
- How do they communicate ideas, understandings, thoughts, and feelings?
- What does their physical behavior suggest?

The goal is not just to label students in terms of intelligences but to develop a textured understanding of how individual students learn, what they bring to the table, where they struggle, and what helps them overcome struggles to persevere—so as to inform planning and curriculum building, for both individuals and groups of students.

Researchers at Project Spectrum (a collaboration between Harvard and Tufts universities) developed activities and observational checklists to help teachers of young students recognize students' intelligences. This delineation helps teachers make sense of key aspects of a domain with which they may not be familiar (Krechevsky & Seidel, 1998, p. 24). In many teacher education programs, teachers now use observation and interviews as part of child or adolescent case studies they conduct, finding student strengths, drawing on them in instruction, and watching the results (see, e.g., Darling-Hammond, 2006).

A few cautions are in order: Teachers must also be careful to avoid the "pigeonholing effect"—labeling students forever as "X" types of learners. All individuals possess certain *combinations* of the various intelligences, and they can apply these differently in different contexts. We can look for specialized strengths in individuals and use them to assist learning, but attaching a permanent label can discourage future success in "weak" areas. Each person has potential in all of the intelligences and it is important to understand that children's intelligences grow and vary over time and contexts (Hatch, 1997).

Another critical point in teacher education is that the student's preferred (already developed) intelligences should not become the medium for all of the student's work in place of developing other needed abilities. Teachers need to be taught to help learners use their preferred entry points as bridges to other skills and broader understandings. A student who has well-developed ability in the spatial domain should not always be encouraged to create visual representations instead of writing. Linguistic skills need to be developed as well. Similarly, a student's interest and proficiency in music may provide a topic for an essay or the background for writing the essay, but should not become a substitute for learning to write proficiently.

That being said, the past 25 years of using MI theory in the classroom have demonstrated that the more information teachers obtain about what students know and think as well as how they learn, the more capacity the former have to reform their pedagogy, and the more opportunities they create for student success.

Providing Powerful Points of Entry

MI theory offers us several ways of thinking about how to introduce, clarify, and help students make sense of new material. In *The Disciplined Mind*, Gardner (1999) describes how teachers can reach diverse students by introducing and presenting rich topics in a different ways, for example, the following:

- By providing powerful *points of entry*—different ways to introduce and approach a topic
- By offering apt *analogies*—connecting new topics to ideas and concepts that are more readily familiar to students
- By providing *multiple representations* of the central or core ideas of the topic

Many of the same strategies are discussed in descriptions of how good teachers use well-developed pedagogical content knowledge (e.g., Shulman, 1987) that is grounded in an understanding of cognition and learning, as well as the central concepts of the disciplines.

Rather than introducing topics only through a lecture, chapter overview, or demonstration of a rule, teachers can use narrative, numerical, aesthetic, and hands-on *points of entry*. A narrative entry point to the study of evolution might tell the story of a single branch on an evolutionary tree or describe the concept of democracy by telling the story of its beginning in ancient Greece (Gardner, 1993). To use a quantitative entry point, students might enter a unit on evolution by analyzing a map that shows the number of different species existing in different geographic areas, or they could be introduced to a unit on Mayan culture by considering population shifts over time. An aesthetic approach to introducing new material might involve watching a movie that introduces a historic event, discussing artwork of a specific period, or responding to poetry read aloud. A hands-on point of entry would provide opportunities for students first to manipulate and explore materials—weights and levers, computer simulations, or the fur of different animals—before launching into a unit of study.

These strategies are now becoming widely used by excellent teachers. For example, video examples of great teachers using all these approaches are now available in collections such as *The Learning Classroom* and the Carnegie Foundation for the Advancement of Teaching's *Quest* Scholars program.[2]

Analogies provide a different kind of hook in introducing new information. They attempt to create a bridge between students' current understanding and the new material to be learned. According to Gardner, "Stripped down, analogies are simply examples drawn from another realm of experience, a realm presumably more familiar to the students than the topic at hand" (1999, p. 199). In science, for example, one can compare the human eye to a camera, the heart to a pump, or a cell to a factory. Although each analogy is limited to a certain extent, offering a similar situation, an evocative image, or a narrative plot can help students begin to grapple with complex subject matter. One science teacher, for example, has found students begin to understand deeply when they are asked to develop the analogy of a cell to a factory and then explain both how the analogy is useful and where it is flawed, thus drawing on what the students know and helping them learn to develop much finer distinctions and reasoning.

And, finally, introducing and encouraging *multiple representations* of the same core ideas can also help learners with differing strengths find their own ways into new material. The same idea can often be thought of in many different ways. The eight intelligences can help us think about a variety of ways an idea may be represented. For instance, the same algebra problem can be discussed in linguistic terms (through a verbal description), mathematical terms (with numerical symbols), and spatial terms (with a graph of the relationships represented). Similarly, the plot of a novel can be described verbally or mapped out visually with a diagram of the relationships between characters. Teachers are now learning about how to select and use representations in increasingly thoughtful and systematic ways, taking these possibilities into account.

Creating Integrated Curriculum and Performances of Understanding

The intelligences are pathways or entry points to understanding, not ends in and of themselves. More important is for teachers to be clear about teaching and learning goals. There are many ways a teacher can incorporate multiple intelligences in the service of understanding. In a *Learning Classroom* videotape about MI in the classroom, for example, teachers in a first- and second-grade class aim for their students to understand the structure of flowers, including the names and functions of different parts. Students read about and dissect flowers, build a model, teach each other what they have learned, and write about flowers, among other strategies. This approach demonstrates to students that understanding means being able to think about an idea in more than one way. In a high school classroom, the teacher asked his students to develop an understanding of the 1970s in terms of the history, culture, politics, social movements, and economic forces at play. Students draw on different intelligences as they research, discuss, write, and develop artistic and dramatic presentations.

Educators have developed many ways to build on MI strategies in the classroom. An innovative mathematics curriculum, for example, leads into a set of algebra lessons with a story about the journey of a group of Western settlers that sets a narrative, historical context in which mathematical problems to be worked through will be set. These problems have authentic purposes, such as calculating how long a quantity of food or water will last and how much should be taken. Teachers may teach graphing both spatially and kinesthetically by using artifacts from the narrative in a role-play context (loading up the wagon with food items and unloading them as time passes and they are used), before teaching graphing in more traditional abstract ways. When learning is integrated, it comes alive and allows problem-focused approaches that are more authentic and can deepen understanding.

Apprenticeships in the arts, sports, crafts, humanities, or applied mathematics and science can allow students to gain expertise in a skill area by working with professional members in their communities. At the Key School in Indianapolis, for example, teachers, parents, and community members mentor students in 17 crafts or disciplines (Campbell, 1997). Groups of students work with these mentors four times a week on topics such as city planning, aerospace, and vocal music. Local museums and industries can also offer student apprenticeships based on real-world tasks and focused on a particular intelligence or discipline. These apprenticeships—like most real-life work—are by their nature interdisciplinary, relying on more than one intelligence for the successful completion of projects and products.

Learning through longer-term, integrated projects, students can conduct multifaceted inquiries into class topics, such as a study of local birds and their nesting habits or research on current issues in local government. When assessments are carried out in the context of a project, multiple intelligences can be tapped. For instance, as part of a project researching water quality in the community, students might create a public service brochure to describe and report what they learned, involving linguistic, logical-mathematical, visual-spatial, and interpersonal skills. The more authentic the task, the more intelligences are drawn on, but also the deeper and more applied the learning.

As Campbell (1997) observed in her study of multiple intelligences classrooms, opportunities for in-depth, self-directed learning also help prepare students for the world beyond school by teaching them how to manage complex projects: "Students learn to ask researchable questions; to identify varied resources; to create realistic time lines; and to initiate, implement, and bring closure to a learning activity" (p. 4).

These projects create opportunities for authentic assessment that allows learning to be displayed in complex, multifaceted ways. Educators have learned that public presentations of such learning, evaluated by teachers, peers, and outside experts against standards of thinking and performance, can stimulate greater motivation and deeper learning. Such exhibitions of learning tap multiple intelligences and provide opportunities for students to share what they have learned through several communication modes. They also promote the development of schoolwide standards that are widely understood, and they encourage greater rigor, as students are encouraged to revise their work to meet standards.

When students' portfolios and products are evaluated by the students themselves, their peers, and their teachers, every member of the school community receives a steady stream of feedback about what quality work looks like. Teachers learn about the success of their curriculum and gain insights about individual students. This system of assessment makes the act of teaching itself an act of professional development, because teachers continually analyze student responses and use them in the development of their pedagogy. The press to cover content is replaced by a press to support students in successful learning, with extraordinary results for student outcomes (Darling-Hammond, Ancess, & Falk, 1995; Darling-Hammond, Ancess, & Ort, 2002).

Such assessments also frequently offer the benefit of tracking growth and development over time. For instance, in a number of schools across the country, seniors must complete a graduation portfolio. Each student is asked to show achievement in literature, history, mathematics, and science and also demonstrate accomplishment in fine arts exhibits and critiques, community service, ethics and social issues, and a physical challenge (Darling-Hammond, Ancess, & Ort, 2002). Gardner (1993) also proposes the idea of a "processfolio," an activity that gives students an opportunity to include *both* finished and unfinished work and to reflect on the many different skills and abilities they used to complete certain products. We have seen that this can be very powerful for students in becoming aware of what they are learning both for guiding their own learning and skill development and for motivating ongoing learning.

A number of studies have found increases in performance on both traditional standardized tests and performance measures for students in classrooms that offer a problem-oriented curriculum that regularly features performance assessment. For example, in a study of more than 2,000 students within 23 restructured schools, Newmann, Marks, and Gamoran

(1995) found much higher levels of achievement on complex performance tasks for students who experienced what these researchers termed "authentic pedagogy"—integrated instruction focused on active learning in real-world contexts calling for higher-order thinking, problem solving with consideration of alternatives, extended writing, and an audience for student work. A recent analysis of the National Education Longitudinal Study (NELS) data found that students in restructured schools where "authentic instruction" was widespread experienced greater achievement gains (Lee, Smith, & Croninger, 1995).

MI theory has supported this kind of work, not only through its approach to thinking about how children learn and how best to teach them, but also through its emphasis on the importance of the variety of skills and performance abilities necessary to succeed in today's world. This contribution of MI theory is critically important for education today. We are accustomed to hearing how the knowledge demands of the society and economy are increasing, and schools are urged to teach lists of skills such as framing and solving problems, accessing, analyzing, and using a wide range of resources, cooperating in producing new ideas and products. We also know that today's society requires many kinds of inventions, from computer programs and other technology solutions to new ways of applying mathematics, science, and humanities understandings in solving problems of the environment, education, and other fields.

However, many current policies hold the traditional school curriculum in place with mandated curriculum based on the ideas of the Committee of Ten in 1890 and with external tests that boil down each domain to a list of facts to be acquired and reproduced, typically from a multiple choice list. These notions of knowledge and learning are increasingly remote from the abilities people need to have to succeed in today's world. Indeed, under current policy contexts, we risk having most of our "Schools Left Behind" by the straitjackets such policies provide.

In the years ahead, MI theory and the fundamental assumptions it brings to the job of education will be even more important in helping us survive and succeed in a world where many highly developed talents and abilities will be essential for human progress.

NOTES

1. This work is more fully described, with videos of teaching practice, in a course series developed by Linda Darling-Hammond and produced by Annenberg/Corporation for Public Broadcasting, *The Learning Classroom: Theory into Practice,* one session of which is devoted to multiple intelligences in the classroom. The series can be viewed at: http://www.learner.org/channel/courses/learningclassroom/.

2. The Learning Classroom is available at http://www.learner.org/channel/ courses/learningclassroom/, and the Carnegie Quest site is at http://gallery .carnegiefoundation.org/insideteaching/quest/collections.html.

REFERENCES

Campbell, L. (1997). Variations on a theme: How teachers interpret MI theory. *Educational Leadership, 55*(1), 14–19.

Darling-Hammond, L. (2006). *Powerful teacher education: Lessons from exemplary programs.* San Francisco: Jossey-Bass.

Darling-Hammond, L., Ancess, J., & Falk, B. (1995). *Authentic assessment in action: Studies of schools and students at work.* New York: Teachers College Press.

Darling-Hammond, L., Ancess, J., & Ort, S. (2002, Fall). Reinventing high school: Outcomes of the coalition campus schools project. *American Educational Research Journal, 39*(3), 639–673.

Gardner, H. (1983). *Frames of mind: The theory of multiple intelligences.* New York: Basic Books.

Gardner, H. (1993). *Multiple intelligences: The theory in practice.* New York: Basic Books.

Gardner, H. (1999). *The disciplined mind.* New York: Simon and Schuster.

Glaser, R. (1990). *Testing and assessment: O tempora! o mores!* Pittsburgh: University of Pittsburgh, Learning Research and Development Center.

Hatch, T. (1997). Getting specific about multiple intelligences. *Educational Leadership, 54*(6), 26–29.

Kornhaber, M., Fierros, E., & Veenema, S. (2003). *Multiple intelligences: Best ideas from research and practice.* New York: Allyn & Bacon.

Krechevsky, M., & Seidel, S. (1998). Minds at work: Applying multiple intelligences in the classroom. In R. J. Sternberg & W. M. Williams (Eds.), *Intelligence, instruction, and assessment: Theory into practice* (pp. 17–42). Mahwah, NJ: Lawrence Erlbaum Associates.

Lee, V. E., Smith, J. B., & Croninger, R. G. (1995, Fall). Another look at high school restructuring. In *Issues in restructuring schools.* Madison: University of Wisconsin-Madison, Center on Organization and Restructuring of Schools.

National Research Council. (1982). *Ability testing: Uses, consequences, and controversies.* Alexandra K. Wigdor & Wendell R. Garner (Eds.). Washington, DC: National Academy Press.

Newmann, F. M., Marks, H. M., & Gamoran, A. (1995). *Authentic pedagogy: Standards that boost student performance.* Issue Report No. 8. Madison, WI: Center on Organization and Restructuring of Schools.

Shulman, L. S. (1987). Knowledge and teaching: Foundations of the new reform. *Harvard Educational Review, 57*(1), 1–22.

Sternberg, R. J. (1997, March). What does it mean to be smart? *Educational Leadership, 54*(6), 20–24.

Tyack, D. B. (1974). *The one best system: A history of American urban education.* Cambridge, MA: Harvard University Press.

CHAPTER 9

On the 25th Anniversary of Multiple Intelligences

Maxine Greene

I feel privileged to have been invited to contribute to this symposium. It happens that I am an educational philosopher with a particular interest in aesthetic education and the development of social imagination. I can say little about the validity or verifiability of Howard Gardner's theories; but I certainly agree with his identification of the failings of public schools. Moreover, I have been stimulated and enriched by contact with his mind, through both reading his books and articles and attending with great interest to his lectures. And I have been awed for a long time by the range of his attainments—from the piano to Chinese art education, from Project Zero to Reggio Emilia, from neuroscience to the several arts.

Like John Dewey and Howard Gardner, I make a distinction between schooling and education. Schooling refers to an institutional undertaking directed to the initiation of groups or classes of the young into what is understood to be the culture, and to equipping them with the skills and knowledge presumably required by the society. Education is, or ought to be, a process of enabling young people to become different, to learn how to make sense of their lived worlds, how to look through the perspectives provided by the disciplines as they order and expand their experience. As Dr. Gardner's work has made clear, the intelligence available to different individuals is many-faceted and distinctive. He has identified, as is well known by now, eight types of intelligences that differ in strength from person to person and in the ways they are put to use in solving problems and doing assigned tasks.

That means that differences in multiple intelligences (MI) profiles should be taken into account and that testing should be done in a variety of ways. Considering the constriction of learning experiences by the high-stakes testing now in use, the very idea of multiple intelligences presents a serious challenge to those who believe that only quantitative measures (the same for all children) can be depended upon in evaluating and comparing achievements.

The present restiveness with respect to testing and the linking of test results to the supposed competency of teachers is an indication of dissatisfaction with the schools in their present state; yet the public thus far has not been equipped to propose alternatives. It is as if the original focus of a common school appointed to teach all children in the same way to comply with the moral laws and master the ABCs has been made into an official curriculum much like a secular catechism.

Dr. Gardner stresses the role of psychology and the social sciences in making the schools how most of them are today. It is interesting to find John Dewey, almost a century ago, calling attention to the same phenomenon. He wrote that the results of the efforts exerted by psychologists and social scientists did not equal the hard work done. This was the result, he went on, of "the lack of imagination in generating leading ideas." For all the quality of the work being done," he said, "we are afraid of speculative ideas, we do over and over again an immense amount of specialized work in the region of 'facts.' We forget that such facts are only data; that is are only fragmentary, uncompleted meanings; and unless they are rounded out into complete ideas—a work that can only be done by hypotheses, by a free imagination of intellectual possibilities—they are as helpless as all maimed things and as repellent as needlessly thwarted events."

The research done by Gardner and his colleagues does take into account the fact that thinking always moves ahead, that all modes of intelligence avoid fixity. I have always been impressed by Dewey's concern for a heightened awareness as an aspect of intelligence in all domains and by his objection to the "anaesthetic" as an aspect of mind—mind thought of as a verb, he said, not a noun, mind as a way of acting in the world. Existentialist as I am, I wish there were more emphasis on choice and action in Gardner's significant work, even as I wish he had dealt with imagination in more depth, and not solely with its centrality in the arts. Also I think he has more to tell us about the kinds of learning that has recently become evident in young people's coming together in campaigns for civil rights and equity in their classrooms and communities.

Since this is a kind of celebration as well as an anniversary of Howard Gardner's work on multiple intelligences, I choose to congratulate him and cheer him on from the vantage point of one as concerned about the study of experience as she is about the ambiguities of existence. I am grateful for his consideration of the ninth kind of intelligence, existential, and feel less than a stranger and more like a fond colleague.

FURTHER READING

Dewey, J. (1938). *Experience and education.* New York: Collier Books.

Greene, M. (1995). *Releasing the imagination: Essay; on education, the arts, and social change.* San Francisco: Jossey-Bass.

Pinar, W. (Ed.) (1998). *The passionate mind of Maxine Greene: 'I am . . . not yet.'* Bristol, PA: Falmer Press, Taylor & Francis.

A View of Multiple Intelligences
from the Principal's Desk

Deborah Meier

One problem with being in the midst of full-time classroom practice for 43 years is that I missed a lot. As a result, many people's influence on me has come in a roundabout way, not through a careful reading of all their work, or trying to clearly think through my agreements and disagreements in a collegial setting. And surely not in the kind of rigorous discourse that so many of the topics deserved. The work of Howard Gardner falls into that category.

I say all this because I'm a sporadic user—in the best and worst sense—of Howard Gardner's many works, but a regular "user" of his message, probably borrowing what I liked best (often without giving credit), and missing some of his deeper and more extended ideas.

All this is to explain (apologize?) for the following thoughts.

We all owe Howard Gardner an enormous debt of gratitude precisely because he has found a way to combine a very respected reputation as a scholar and academician with a deceptively "easy" and accessible idea that served us unusually well. The critics of IQ tests have been many, and they include both scholars and practitioners. But few have found a way to present their ideas as usefully. Gardner filled an empty place. If one was against the way IQ was being used to disparage whole groups of our fellow beings, as well as mislead us into ignoring the talents of so many of our children, we were always faced with the inevitable desire to acknowledge that "somehow," "someway," "surely" even we egalitarians had to admit, not everyone was equally good at everything and that some folks were "smarter" and some "dumber." In the absence of another way to organize talents, this (the traditional IQ) would have to do. We objected, but ineffectually. I referred folks to books, chapters, essays—but it was hard to summarize them convincingly. So I resorted to stories. This method worked if I had time enough, at least for those who trusted me.

Today I merely have to glibly refer to "multiple intelligences" to make my point.

Knocking down an existing paradigm is hard enough, unless one has on hand an alternative one; and best of all one that appears to have a hard, scientific basis—and ideally one with a quick and catchy way to summarize its findings.

Gardner used the language of the field of academia to question the assumptions of academics. After all, the people who read and write scholarly books are prone naturally to see themselves well served by the usual ways to assess talent and to see their own kind of intelligence as the coin of the realm. Sometimes they acknowledge having been poor test takers and thus were mislabeled in their early years. But it was, they assume, a fluke, and in the end the same measures have proved otherwise. They deserve their esteemed status. The IQ test is a kind of Wizard of Oz, conferring genius on the fit.

In that battle Gardner was always on "our" side—if not in all particulars (he had his own ideas about the best way to reform schools), in the general direction he pointed us in. If I have had any doubts about the science of it all, that's because I have doubts about most educational science. It's not out of an antiscientific habit of mind, but quite the opposite—or so I would argue. Even where there is general consensus on what constitutes our goals, we are often hard put to be sure that what we espouse is Science, rather than "merely" our best effort to use scientific thinking to come to a tentative "best" recommendation. I speak here of medicine and nutrition, of course—not just education. In the field of education, where ends themselves are not easily or obviously something we can agree on—filled as they are with our own values and politics—measurement becomes even trickier and science more problematic. Intelligence and "giftedness" fall precisely into this tricky realm. And to complicate matters more fully, as in medicine, what is innate and what depends upon one's environment—including schooling itself—is far from a settled matter. Yet in some way, including Gardner's, there is a presumption that we come "wired" in one way or another—toward one "g" or many "gs."

Of course, in reality the concept that Gardner put forth is not as simple as we "users" pretended, nor as uncontroversial, or even—for our own uses—as unproblematic. I have finally begun to read more carefully much of Gardner's work, and finding myself more comfortable with much of it, as well as uncomfortable with others. But the debt I owe him is not trivial or, I hope, taken in the wrong way. To place our ideas into the field in ways that enable us to "make use" of them is not to be dismissed as a PR trick. I've sometimes argued, in fact, that one should receive a doctorate not for writing a dissertation that is unlikely to influence anyone, but for demonstrating that one's work can and should be influential to the field in which it is a part. The phrase "the having of wonderful ideas" was used for the title of a book by fellow Harvard professor Eleanor Duckworth. It's a marvelous book, but the title alone has sustained me over the years as a way of thinking about the purposes of schooling. We need these phrases, expressions of belief and conviction.

There may be five, six, seven, or eventually eight, nine, or ten forms of intelligence that Gardner can demonstrate convincingly. The breakthrough for me is that there is more than one—and I would suspect in fact a different one for each and every child that's born. We can sort them into prefixed, precoded categories, but in the end the critical point is that we need to respectfully and closely observe each other and avoid categorization and labeling altogether.

Of course, language itself is a form of labeling, and so the goal I've set—of thinking, as parents and teachers, about each child as a unique entity—is always just out of reach. Any description based on words or even pictures suggests a generalization of some sort.

Still, I want to preserve the idea that it's our unique mixture of experiences and "ways of seeing the world" that can never be entirely unwrapped and defined. But it's that uniqueness that we need to meet, join with, as educators. The "thee, thou, and it" of David Hawkins's marvelous triangle ends up being a particular "thee," a particular "thou," and a particular "it."

Broadening our capacity to think about our fellow humans is at the heart of the educator's task—no matter what field he or she practices in, including politics, the academy, or the schoolhouse. Few of us have had a greater impact on this than Howard Gardner, even if I shall never be quite convinced that the seven intelligences are any more scientific than the single old-fashioned one. (Embarrassingly enough, as I write these words, New York City's Department of Education—read "Mayor Bloomberg"—has decided to use the old single IQ test to map the future schooling of all children, starting at age 4, who enter the 1.2 million-student system! Howard: there's work to be done. We need you here at home in NYC.)

It's being proposed, by the NYC Department of Education, in the name of equity. The idea that IQ tests should be a tool on behalf of equity is hard to swallow and makes me wonder where Chancellor Klein and Bloomberg have been for the past century. Probably not involved in educational issues. For if there was any single schooling tool that misserved the poor, immigrants, and people of color, the IQ test was the worst. Starting a century or more ago, it justified the view that eastern Europeans, Jews, and even southern Europeans were inferior races. Yes, the word *race* was used to describe them. It went without saying in those days that people of color were even lower in the scale of human intelligence. The method for arriving at this conclusion was a test designed in a circular fashion—the qualities of mind that could be teased out of paper-and-pencil tests for separating people in the higher professions from the lower forms of labor were obviously those that defined intelligence. It was more complicated, as psychometricians developed complex tables and curves to buttress their arguments, but underlying them were "hard data"—answers people gave to questions asked them. It was better, as Stephen Jay Gould pointed out in *The Mismeasure of Man*, than mismeasuring their craniums, which was the predecessor of IQ tests for defining human intelligence. It separated humans in an inconvenient way, when the measurements were carefully redone in a more impartial way.

Having grown up in a Jewish family and community, I quickly realized that the criteria was absurd. And when a friend of mine tested my oldest son's IQ, I was convinced. Not because he had a low one, but because it was the first time I discovered what kind of questions formed the basis of the decisions, and this particular son turned out to be very hard to classify (he scored better on the more advanced questions, and poorly on the easier ones!). Under normal testing circumstances the test giver might never have got to the ones my son delighted in answering correctly.

Intuitively, as a teacher and mother, I realized that if I described even my own three children, I would be describing quite different ways of taking in the world and organizing it for their own purposes and pleasures. Depending on what assortment of qualities I might put together, they would each come out on top—depending on which choices I made. I could easily design it to favor any one of the three.

I thought about how dumb I might have appeared had I been born in China, with its emphasis on detailed memorization of quantities of text. I could barely memorize more than a simple kindergarten song—even with the help of music. My rote memory is one of my very weakest skills. I'm not boasting; it has cost me. But I found other ways to accumulate knowledge and put together ideas, and I decided to turn it into a strength. I get away with it most of the time. Someone told me recently that there's a name for it—nominal aphasia.

I also have a poor capacity for "tone"—for being able to translate a sound I have in my head to one I can repeat; and it hasn't helped me in my desire to be a good pianist or singer, not out of lack of interest, but because I gave up earlier than others in frustration at what seemed so much easier to them than to me. It got embarrassing at piano concerts when children younger than me with fewer years of lessons were playing much more complex pieces and doing it more musically. I dropped out.

Could I have, as some would argue, learned to be good at both—memorizing and music—had I had more open-minded teachers and been willing to tolerate failure and frustration? Surely that's more than possible, even likely. But probably at a cost—and one I "chose" not to pay. I often have second thoughts about it, when one or the other sorely interferes with the pleasures of life.

It's truly hard to not remember the names of close acquaintances—people who have every reason to think I'm a friend. Surely politics was not going to be the right career move for me. And whenever I listen to a friend, much less a real concert pianist, play, I realize that had I not given up, playing even half as well as they do would have given me such pleasure. The ability to produce such sounds with one's own body seems to me the ultimate joy. How could one ever be depressed for long if one could do that?

But then I worried. Would Gardner's approach close off such possibilities even more? By classifying, would we rest easier in depriving me of a musical education? Would we start a new search for where we ranked in all eight intelligences and develop a score that included all of them? Or would we decide to weight them all in different ways—with "verbal/logical" at the top?

What "scientific" basis is there for doing so? Or would it matter?

And how can schools, parents, and society settle instead for having none of these measures, or leaving it a very loose and "soft science," with a focus on each of being more tolerant of each other's variant talents, skills, abilities, intelligences—that are in the end best "tested" in real life performances?

In the end, the schools I was involved in sought the latter solution. We looked for overlapping habits that we thought were probably true, if requiring some rewording, of all Gardner's eight intelligences, plus maybe more. We called these the "five habits of mind." We squeezed in habits of heart with them, and then built a process for demonstrating one's work that required strong work habits. Over and over again we "demanded" that young people "show us" their stuff in a variety of disciplines and field of interest, and we assessed them in a face-to-face way, by a committee of both near and far experts—folks who knew the student well and those who did not know them at all, except through their work. Just as a musician's real test is an audition, a visual artist's a showing of his or her work, so would student's preparation for the next stage of life be measured by performance—auditions of sort.

But I forget as I propose this that it does not satisfy a lot of people I respect. They want what Gardner has offered—a system, an "objective" tool for judging them. If we could apply that to their performances (and we try, through what we call protocols or rubrics) they might buy it. But the beauty of auditions is precisely that, in the end, taste matters; subjective response counts. A manuscript turned down by eight publishers finally finds a ninth that publishes it to critical acclaim.

It's those stories of perseverance and triumph against the odds that I want to make schools honor and young people esteem. The purpose of schools is to "beat the odds," not to confirm our limited capacities for making predictions. It's also (but that's another subject) in a way, the unscientific premise upon which democracy rests—our faith in one person, one vote, and all that underlies that sentimental idea.

Gardner's work opens up these claims and possibilities for more of us, but I want it wider still—even if hard-nosed Science doesn't back me up.

FURTHER READING

Gould, S. J. (1981). *The mismeasure of man.* New York: Norton.

Hawkins, D. (1995). *Power vs. force, the hidden determinants of human behavior: An anatomy of consciousness.* West Sedona, AZ: Veritas.

Meier, D. (1995). *The power of their ideas: Lessons from a small school in Harlem.* Boston: Beacon Press.

Meier, D. (2002). *In schools we trust: Creating communities of learning in an era of testing and standardization.* Boston: Beacon Press.

Meier, D. (2004). *Many children left behind: How the No Child Left Behind Act is damaging our children and our schools.* Boston: Beacon Press.

CHAPTER 11

Multiple Intelligences in My Life

Ellen Winner

When Branton Shearer asked me to write about how Howard Gardner's theory of multiple intelligences has affected my life, I agreed, but only reluctantly. My reluctance was because my relationship to MI theory is so personal. As Jane Eyre says at the end of the novel, "Reader, I married him." Howard Gardner is my husband, so I am married to MI theory. But in fact I knew Howard long before MI theory was born, when he was fresh out of graduate school and defining himself as a researcher studying artistic abilities as they developed in children and as they broke down under conditions of brain damage.

As Howard studied artistic abilities in children and in brain-damaged patients, he began to notice children who were prodigies but only in one particular art form, and stroke victims who lost one artistic capacity but nothing else. I know he was musing for quite a while about how Piaget must have been wrong in thinking of cognitive development as a unitary kind of thing. And I recall Howard in his early 30s telling me that someday he wanted to write a book on "kinds of minds." *Someday*, for Howard, tends to mean very soon, and I witnessed a file folder quickly fattening as he kept stuffing it with notes on different kinds of minds. Within a short span of time, this idea had morphed into kinds of intelligences.

Perhaps Howard's own jagged profile of intelligences contributed to the need to write a book about MI. Not everyone knows that Howard is color blind but has perfect pitch. Both these characteristics are rare; one is considered a defect, the other a "gift." Despite being color blind, Howard's favorite 20th-century artist is the color field painter Mark Rothko—and yet every morning I have to tell Howard if his clothes match. It makes perfect sense that someone so gifted and also so handicapped would realize that MI was the theory to develop. (Of course, I know that MI is not about sensory abilities but about operations on sensory materials.)

There are other amusing ways in which Howard's profile is uneven. For instance, Howard is somewhat clumsy (he can't stand on one leg for more than a few seconds; we would never want to see him try to ski!), but he loves to watch ballet. And while he has terrific intrapersonal skills and is a very good analyst of his own strengths and weaknesses, his interpersonal skills sometimes strike me as leaving something to be desired. Howard is a bit oblivious and does not always pick up on subtle nonverbal cues that I notice readily. Once after spending quite a bit of time with another couple, I told Howard that this couple had a bad marriage and I would not be surprised if the marriage did not last. Howard was very surprised, having noticed no tensions. A half year later, the couple separated.

Howard and I have been married since 1982. We were professional collaborators for a number of years. When we began to work together, we studied children's conceptions of the arts, children's understanding of metaphor and irony, brain-damaged patients' understanding of metaphor, and gifted children's development in the arts. But even though we collaborated, our intellectual profiles were not the same, and we complemented each other: I focused more on analysis, Howard on synthesis. For example, in our studies of metaphor and irony, I dissected the processes involved in each form of understanding, while Howard pondered the relationships between various forms of figurative language.

By the middle 1980s, our intellectual paths began to diverge. In 1983, Howard's kinds-of-minds idea appeared as *Frames of Mind*, which he ultimately conceived of as an attack on the construct of intelligence and an attack on the reification of IQ. When this book was championed by educators, Howard began to think more and more about educational issues and, ultimately, about issues in professional ethics. In contrast, I remained in the experimental psychology fold. But even though our work has moved in different directions, we always read each other's work and are often each other's harshest critics.

In the 1990s, I began to focus my work on giftedness in the arts and the relationship between giftedness in the arts and the kind of giftedness more often studied—giftedness in intellectual areas measured by IQ tests. When I began this research, I did not set out to do so from the perspective of multiple intelligences theory. After all, that was my husband's theory, and I hoped to keep my work separate and independent. I found, however, that it was impossible to think about giftedness without at the same time thinking about intelligence. And once I went down this road, I found that I could not quite disentangle my view of giftedness from Howard's theory of MI.

By *giftedness*, I am referring to the high end of an ability or intelligence. There is variability in every kind of human intelligence. Hence, every intelligence has individuals at both the high and the low ends of the spectrum. Thus, any theory of giftedness must be rooted in a theory of human abilities, or human intelligences. As I researched what is known about gifted children, I could not help but be struck by how prodigies seemed to exhibit one or possibly two of the intelligences delineated in *Frames of Mind*: Prodigies in math, reading, athletics, visual art, music abound. Rarely did I encounter a globally gifted prodigy. In fact, I came to realize that "globally gifted" really meant gifted in all school-type subjects, children who had both verbal and mathematical strengths. While there are plenty of these kinds of children, there are also many children far stronger in verbal than mathematical abilities, or the reverse. And virtually never did I encounter a child strong in both of these skills and also strong in visual arts and music and athletics.

Like Howard, I had been profoundly influenced by the work of the behavioral neurologist Norman Geschwind. I was fascinated by his concept of "pathology of superiority," in which he described individuals with spatial talents and verbal deficits. Many of the gifted children I studied fit this picture to a T: children with extraordinary spatial abilities who had difficulty learning to read. And so, as I wrote my book on gifted children, *Gifted Children: Myths and Realities*, though I struggled against fitting my findings into a MI framework, I could not manage not to. The data just fit the MI model too well.

I have often been struck by how the gifted education community has misinterpreted multiple intelligences theory. There is a pervasive feeling that Howard has attacked the very heart and concept of giftedness. The argument goes, fallaciously, as follows: If there are multiple intelligences, then all children are gifted in at least one of the intelligences; therefore all children are gifted. Naturally, those who are arguing for the need for resources for the traditionally defined gifted are not going to be pleased by the argument that all children are gifted. However, there is absolutely nothing in Gardner's theory that leads to the conclusion that all children are strong in at least one of the intelligences. To be sure, if there is more than one way to be intelligent, more children will be classified as gifted than if there is only one (IQ) way. But following from MI theory, it is of course possible to be weak in all the intelligences. At the most, people have relative strengths.

And so, multiple intelligences has permeated my life. It's impossible to steer clear of this theory, I find, because it makes so much common sense, and because confirmatory examples are so common. Howard's jagged profile complements mine. His high intrapersonal intelligence is balanced by my high interpersonal intelligence; he is musical, but I'm tone deaf; I was a painter, he is color blind. We overlap in one intelligence, thank goodness: We are both very verbal, and we can talk well about our disagreements! And we are both logical enough that an argument put forth by one of us can at least upon occasion be refuted by the other.

FURTHER READING

Hetland, L., Winner, E., Veenema, S., & Sheridan, K. (2007). *Studio thinking: The real benefits of visual arts education*. New York: Teachers College Press.

Winner, E. (1982). *Invented worlds: The psychology of the arts*. Cambridge, MA: Harvard University Press.

Winner, E. (1988). *The point of words: Children's understanding of metaphor and irony*. Cambridge, MA: Harvard University Press.

Winner, E. (1996). *Gifted children: Myths and realities*. New York: Basic Books.

CHAPTER 12

Reflections on My Works and Those of My Commentators

Howard Gardner

A Rorschach test that runs 400 pages? It hardly seems likely. Usually, a Rorschach inkblot is an ambiguous configuration spread across one page. Viewers describe what they see, but, of course, their report is principally a projection of their chief preoccupations—one respondent sees a mother hugging a child, a second discerns a husband strangling a wife, a third describes two beasts clawing at one another's innards.

In the early 1980s, after several years of research, I published *Frames of Mind: The Theory of Multiple Intelligences* (Gardner, 1983). In my own mind, the book was a synthesis of many strands of research, a few of which I had conducted myself, most of which I had learned from an examination of scientific and social-scientific literature. With the help of capable colleagues, I had surveyed what was known about human cognition from brain science, evolutionary evidence, anthropological reports, and several lines of psychological research. I proposed that the human mind ought to be construed as a set of relatively independent cognitive capacities that could, of course, work together in numerous ways. In a decision that proved to be crucial, I elected to call these faculties "human intelligences." Chances are, if I had written a book about seven talents or seven competences, the book would have remained in obscurity and you would not be reading these words today.

At the time, I would have said that I saw my synthesis as a response to Piaget, the great psychologist of cognitive development, who saw all intellect as a unitary entity. Secondarily, I would have described my effort as a critique of the conception of intelligence as it has been customarily viewed in psychology, and particularly in psychometrics. Although parts of the book touched on education, I did not consider myself an educator (or educationist) and I did not see my book as a contribution to education.

Authors control the words in their books (and, sometimes, even the titles thereof), but once a book leaves an author's hands, there is little the author can do to control its fate. And this is just as well—an author invariably has several axes to grind and it is by no means certain that the book achieved just what the author intended. We authors are as likely as anyone to commit the "intentionalist fallacy"—to confuse what we intended with what we achieved.

And here I return to the Rorschach: Although in my own mind, I was clear enough about what I wanted to achieve, I did not anticipate the reactions of others. First, as an author of several previous books, I did not think that this book would attract more attention than the others. In this I was wrong—I have written well more than 20 books but none has had the immediate, or the long-term, impact of *Frames of Mind*. As the cliché goes, it changed my life.

Second, I did not anticipate the principal audience. I had seen the book as addressed primarily to my fellow psychologists—especially those in my subdisciplines of developmental psychology, cognitive psychology, and neuropsychology. But most psychologists were not that interested in the book, and influential psychologists who responded to the book were not particularly sympathetic. The critical reactions ranged from "outlandish," to "wrong-headed," to "old hat." All too often, the negative reaction was quite vehement. Never in my previous writings had I stepped heavily on other scholars' toes, but in this case, I clearly had. In particular, the psychometric establishment was up in arms. A theory like mine hit a raw nerve with individuals whose careers are based on belief in a singular intelligence, and its susceptibility to testing by a single, simple-as-possible instrument.

In other parts of the scholarly community, the responses were, perhaps understandably, more muted. After all, I was not goring their oxen. It is worth noting that biologists have often been quite sympathetic to the theory. Unlike most psychological syntheses of the time, mine relied heavily on evidence from biology—particularly from neuroscience and, to a lesser extent, from genetics and evolutionary theory. Also, unlike those in the physical sciences, biologists are accustomed to the often counterintuitive and haphazard ways in which organic systems are arranged. The apparent lack of logical consistency in the names and ranges of the intelligences did not bother most biologists. On the other hand, I found that mathematicians were quite dismissive of the theory. As far as they were concerned, there is only one kind of intelligence—the sort captured in the phrase "logical-mathematical intelligence."

I did notice one wrinkle in the armamentarium of mathematicians. Once aware that his or her child had a learning difficulty, the mathematical parent might become an instant convert to MI theory.

By far the largest audience for MI theory was found among educators. First in the United States, and then in many other countries, the idea of multiple intelligences found a ready and, more often than not, an eager audience. In a way that remains somewhat mysterious even after a quarter century, teachers, principals, and policy makers at various levels resonated with the principal claims of the theory—at least as they understood it.

"As they understood it"—once again, the Rorschach test. Some people saw the book as addressed to those in special education, others as being addressed to gifted children, or to neglected children. Some readers saw the book as an argument for tracking, others as a critique of that practice. Some looked for a rationale for a certain curriculum, others for a form of pedagogy, still others as an argument for new forms of assessment. Of course, the book called for "none of the above"—and, indeed, for a full decade, I remained relatively agnostic on the optimal educational implications and applications of MI theory.

As a dividend, 25 years of speechifying on this topic has yielded several elevator speeches. When I am asked to summarize MI theory in a sentence, I can do so. "Whereas most theorists of intelligence see the human mind as a single, all-purpose computer, I believe the human mind is better construed as a set of relatively independent computational devices—which I have named the 'multiple intelligences.'"

As a bonus, I can now supply the two educational implications that have stood the test of time. In my view, two principal educational implications follow from multiple intelligences theory:

1. Pay attention to individual differences. And to the extent that you can individualize education, do so.
2. Decide on what is really important in your discipline or field and teach it, convey it, in several different ways. By that approach, you can reach more children. Moreover, you demonstrate what it means to have a keen understanding of a topic. Those with such a well-worked out understanding can present the topic in several ways. If you can only present your topic in one way, your grasp of it is likely to be tenuous.

Drawing on his initial idea, his energy, and his organizational capacities, Branton Shearer has collected a fine set of reflections on the idea of multiple intelligences. I'm grateful to Branton for having assembled this collection, which nicely complements a growing literature of accounts and critiques of MI theory (see Chen, Moran, & Gardner, 2009; Gardner, 2006b,

2008; Gardner & Moran, 2006; Schaler, 2006). And I appreciate the opportunity to comment on these reflections.

Upon an initial reading of the contributions to this volume, I was impressed by the great diversity of persons and the equally wide range of their views. Although the Rorschach period has passed, MI theory continues to attract a varied audience with diverse perspectives.

A second pleasure derived from the continuing generativity of the ideas. Even when works of scholarship stir an initial stir, that stir rarely lasts very long. I freely admit that when I first wrote about multiple intelligences, I did not anticipate that I myself would continue to mine these ideas—ultimately writing about education, creativity, leadership, even business from a multiple intelligences perspective (Gardner, 1991, 1993a, 1993b, 1995, 1997, 1999b). Nor did I realize that I myself would increase my understanding of the theory as a courtesy of these explorations. For example, when I initially wrote about multiple intelligences, I did not appreciate the important distinction between intelligences and domains, or the tendency of people to confuse intelligences with learning styles; sensory systems; and noncognitive features such as personality, temperament, or spirituality (Gardner, 1993a, 1999a, 2006a). How gratifying to see that these by now well-known and much discussed ideas continue to stimulate discussion a quarter century later.

A third reaction was an intriguing surprise. I know some of the contributors to the volume very well (I am even married to one of them!), while I have not met or scarcely know others. Yet the degree of familiarity was not a predictor of how positive or negative the reaction was. As a scholar, I am pleased by this outcome. Evaluation of a scholar's work should be founded on the merits, and not on sociometric distance.

So much for general comments. For the sake of convenience, I've divided the commentaries into five categories. I make no claim that these categories are airtight—a different scheme could be used, and some authors could fit into more than one theory. Yet the classification has helped me, and I hope that it will help you as well.

1. MI AS A SCIENTIFIC THEORY

I take both the term *scientific* and the term *science* seriously. Our prototypes of scientific theory come from physics—the physics of Newton, Einstein, and quantum mechanics. The other "hard sciences"—ranging from biology to geology—also have their eyes keyed on physics and perhaps, on occasion, exhibit "physics envy."

I've never thought of psychology as a science in the same sense. Broad theories of psychology—the kind we associate with the writings of William

James, Sigmund Freud, Jean Piaget, and B. F. Skinner—are definitely out of fashion. The parts of psychology in which I am most interested—cognitive psychology, developmental psychology—are more than likely to be absorbed into a broader interdisciplinary undertaking called *cognitive neuroscience*. Workers in that tradition will examine the neural and the mental representations of different skills, capacities, and potentials. The "softer" parts of psychology—in particular, personality, motivation, group behavior—are likely to consist of evocative demonstrations and to be informed as much by relevant literary and artistic works as by standard experimental paradigms.

As for theory, again, the kind of theory associated with the hard sciences seems remote from that encountered in social sciences. I think that the word *framework* is probably a more apt descriptor than the promissory note *theory*. A good social scientific or behavioral scientific framework provides a way of thinking about the world of human behavior and institutions. The four renowned psychologists named above certainly created powerful frameworks, even though nowadays we look to frameworks that cover delimited areas, such as children's conceptions of number, human altruistic behavior, conformity to the group, and the like.

Once one goes beyond elementary sensory and perceptual mechanisms, another feature is peculiar to human sciences. The very articulation of a concept, the facts of an experiment, can exert strong influence on humans who learn about the work. So, as an example, 50 years ago psychoanalyst Erik Erikson described the "identity crisis." Suddenly millions of people all over the world discover that they are undergoing identity crises. But a generation later, perhaps in part because everyone knows about the crisis of identity, adolescents are better described in a different way. Or, as another example, the lamentable human tendency to obey arbitrary authority, as demonstrated dramatically in the famous Milgram experiments of the 1960s, paradoxically causes more individuals to stand up to authority. At least one can hope so.

As Noam Chomsky indicates in his commentary, MI theory falls broadly speaking into the set of ideas that emerged at the time when the influence of behaviorism was waning in American (and other) social sciences. In particular, the cognitive revolution legitimized talk of internal, mental representations; and, in the version made famous by Chomsky, it legitimized a modular approach to cognition, where capacities like language, music, or spatial reasoning were seen as separate, distinct from one another in crucial ways. This work has had ramifications across the scholarly disciplines; it is not too much to say that, when it comes to cognition, we are all Chomskians.

Chomsky discusses briefly the difference between surface and deep structures. These terms have a technical meaning and, in invoking them, it is important not to be misleading. An interesting analogy may be at work with respect to multiple intelligences. In life, we cannot observe intelligences per se at work. Rather we see their surface manifestations—in the tasks that individuals carry out, the domains in which they work, the skills that they exhibit. In any of these cases, inference is required to figure out which underlying intelligences are at work. Analogically speaking, we are then engaged in a search for the deep structure of a human achievement.

Marc Hauser, clearly a Chomskian, does not find my concept of intelligences to be congenial. He prefers to conceive of "core competences" and to investigate how these operate in humans and in primates. Note, however, that one of the eight defining features of intelligence is the existence of a core competence. Hauser and I are on the same page here. Where we differ is in research approach: I post the core competence, confident in the belief that others will probe its units and mode of operation; Hauser is one of numerous scholars, several of them colleagues of ours at Harvard, who have taken it upon themselves to unravel the nature of these core competence and, importantly, their relation or lack of relation to one another.

It is also fair to say that the capacities of interest to Hauser are of a smaller grain size than those captured in the idea of multiple intelligences. Note, however, that each of the intelligences actually is composed of several subintelligences, and these are closer in grain size (and perhaps in brain size!) to those investigated by Hauser and colleagues.

Unknown to one another, Hauser and I have both contrasted "laser" and "searchlight capacities." Hauser compares "laser primates" to "searchlight humans." I instead contrast those human beings, such as artists and scientists, who rely ever more on the deep probing by a single intelligence with those human beings, such as politicians, business managers and leaders, who must focus broadly and, perhaps, use several intelligences.

Hauser indicates that the line of research in which he is engaged is concerned primarily with universals—those capacities shared by all human beings. He contrasts that emphasis with an interest in individual differences, characteristic both of psychometricians and, in another key, of classroom teachers. It is true that our foci are complementary here. But note that all human beings possess the intelligences—in that sense, they are the proposed set of cognitive universals. Hauser agrees that human beings will differ in their strengths and weaknesses, but leaves that study to other disciplines and other disciplinarians.

As a student of the history of science, Chomsky shrewdly depicts the steps necessary for promising or pregnant ideas to enter the solid edifice of science. I agree with him that a mature science requires well-defined terms and concepts; strictly designed methodologies through which the nature of, and relationship between, these terms/concepts can be investigated; criteria by which the results of these methodological inquiries (observations, experiments, case studies) can be judged; procedures whereby the initial theoretical formulation is reformulated in light of new data and new analyses.

Again, while this is standard operating procedure in the established sciences, such a regimen is still in its infancy in the social sciences. Few investigators have made as much progress as Chomsky in proceeding from promising idea to a theoretical edifice of power and a significant degree of acceptance. In that sense, in comparison to linguistic theory, MI theory is in a still-inchoate state, neither I nor my colleagues have done more than sketch the steps that would be necessary to convert it into a plausible science.

Finally, both Chomsky and Hauser put forth some of their own educational ideas, concepts, and practices with which I have some sympathy. They correctly recognize that the branches of science with which they are involved have little as of yet to contribute to educational practice. In that sense MI theory has travelled further.

2. MI AS A CONTRIBUTION TO PSYCHOLOGY

MI theory is avowedly interdisciplinary, and its effects have been felt much more in education than in standard psychology. Still, I am a psychologist and I do approach issues in ways that are more characteristic of psychology than of any other discipline. It is therefore of interest to monitor the reactions of two highly regarded psychologists, Michael Posner and Mihaly Csikszentmihalyi.

As noted above, I originally saw my work as a contribution to cognitive psychology and developmental psychology: an iconoclastic view of how the human mind has developed and how it is organized. I drew heavily on neuroscientific knowledge, a convincing way to establish the plausibility of the particular set of competences that I had identified. Michael Posner has done as much as any psychologist to root his findings in neuroscientific and, increasingly, in genetic evidence. Both in the area of human attentional processes, and, more recently, in his studies of reading, he has delineated the fine structure of these capacities and the ways in which they may vary across individuals. In that sense, Posner's work exemplifies the kinds of fine-grained study of individual intelligences (or, more neutrally, cognitive capacities) that will be needed if MI theory is to be taken seriously in the psychological and cognitive sciences, broadly speaking. His interest in the varying strengths of connectivity among neural networks may well point to a way of assessing the strengths of, and the relations between, the several intelligences. Posner's work is the best response I could provide to the critique offered by Hauser.

It is gratifying to acknowledge Posner's sympathetic view of MI theory. Where Hauser sees it as either wrongheaded or at least tangential to his interests, both Chomsky and Posner are more alert to its potential and less judgmental about its admittedly nascent instantiations. I will leave it to others to determine whether these contrasting judgments are more a matter of taste, seniority, or view of the scientific enterprise.

Once, in an aside, Mihaly Csikszentmihalyi commented to me, "Howard, the cognitive stuff is easy; it's the understanding of motivation that is challenging." Never one to duck a challenge, Csikszentmihalyi has devoted much of his career to an understanding of why humans do what they do, what sorts of activities attract them, why they remain or do not remain with these activities, and what, in the end, the quality of their life experiences is.

Csikszentmihalyi correctly points out that his and my interests and work have been complementary. Perhaps that is a reason why many educators have attended both to the intelligences of their students and to the potential for "flow experiences" in encounters with disparate objects and activities. Certainly, there is no conflict between these two foci; indeed, much could be gained if we could unravel the connections between intellectual profiles, on the one hand, and motivational peaks and valleys, on the other.

While sympathetic to the activation of the range of intelligences, and personally committed to artistic activity and experience, Csikszentmihalyi acknowledges that in the world of today, and perhaps that of tomorrow, linguistic and logical intelligences continue to hold sway. The future power of MI theory lies, he insists, in demonstrating that one can assess the other intelligences and establish their "cash value." In putting forth this view, Csikszentmihaly anticipates the reactions of others who are more centrally involved in traditional views of intelligence.

3. MI AS A RESPONSE TO STANDARD THEORIES OF INTELLIGENCE

In writing *Frames of Mind*, I was not principally concerned with traditional theories of intelligence. That is probably because I did not have training in the psychology of intelligence and was only distantly familiar with that specialty before launching the research that led to the book. But I soon learned that the study of intelligence is a very crowded area in psychology, that it has very strong advocates, that its influence in education continues to be tremendous, and that empirical data purporting to demystify the explanatory power of "g" and "IQ" continues to accumulate, both in psychology and in relevant biological sciences.

I am pleased, therefore, that Charles Murray and James Flynn, both major contributors to the literature on intelligence, have contributed to this symposium. Citing a surprising encomium from Arthur Jensen, Murray seeks to introduce some calmness to the discussion. He suggests that we speak of abilities or capacities, rather than intelligences. While insisting on the current valuing of language and logic (and perhaps spatial capacities), he acknowledges that different abilities have been honored in different eras and sites. He makes the useful distinction between a focus on the individual, where unique profiles of intelligences are of high importance, and a focus on policy, where broader patterns of abilities and disabilities continue to hold sway.

Readers of Murray over the years, and I am one, will recognize this voice as softer and more congenial than that sometimes encountered in his provocative books and op-ed pieces. (Perhaps the coexistence in one body/ mind of two rhetorical personae is a characteristic of many contributors to this volume, including me.) It is possible that my Harvard classmate Charles Murray and I may be closer to one another than was the case 15 years ago, when he coauthored *The Bell Curve* (Herrnstein & Murray, 1994) and I responded critically to the book, in writing, on the air, and in a live debate. Here's to the wisdom of the ages!

Using my writings as a point of departure, James Flynn has written a sensitive essay—one in which he puts forth his own current thinking about the enterprise in which we have both been engaged over the years. Taking his broad stand with the history of work in this area, he delineates an area called "cognitive intelligence" and identifies as its defining feature the capacity to hold a wide range of concepts/ideas/schemas in mind simultaneously and successively. While in formulation this sounds suspiciously like the contents of an IQ test, Flynn goes on to make a further distinction: Within domains like art or sports or politics, one can distinguish between those individuals who have high skills (in my terms, high intelligences) and those who can think in sophisticated ways about them whether or not they have the same high level of the skill per se (thereby exhibiting high cognitive intelligence in that realm). I find these distinctions useful: One might say, the difference between a high intelligence and a high metaintelligence.

Departing somewhat from the topic at hand, Flynn offers his own thoughts about the words or concepts we should use in characterizing people; whether we should rank them, and if so, how; whether we should share these rankings with the individuals themselves. While a self-described humanist, he is a conservative in the use of language and prefers to retain a more constrained connotation for the word *intelligence*. He says that each culture necessarily has a hierarchy of roles and skills and we should simply accept this fact, without making unnecessarily odious comparisons.

Before writing *Frames of Mind* I would probably have concurred with Flynn's general thoughts as well as those put forth by of Csikszentmihalyi. But now, perhaps making a virtue of necessity, I see the value of using (and pluralizing) the word *intelligence* and am glad that I did. Only by such a lexical stretch was it possible to challenge the individuals who thought that they owned and could operationalize intelligence just as they chose; and only by such a lexical stretch could ordinary persons (often victims of the use of the promiscuous word *intelligence*) broaden their own views of cognition and mind. Moreover, even if it is the case that we will continue to valorize "cognitive intelligence," we should be aware that that is what we are doing—and we should be open to envisioning a society in which alternative value(s) and rank orderings are possible. Indeed, it is just possible that when computers have surpassed most examples of human cognitive intelligence, we will prioritize or at least remain open to a different conception of mind. If MI theory can contribute to that possibility, so much the better.

4. MI AS EDUCATIONAL THEORY AND PRACTICE

As I've stressed a number of times, MI theory does not in and of itself make any firm educational recommendations—hence the opening image of the Rorschach test. And indeed, there are no strong reasons in my own background for espousing one kind of educational philosophy as opposed to another. In Scranton, Pennsylvania, at the middle of the last century, I went to quite traditional schools; only when I attended Harvard College in the early 1960s did I become aware of the range of educational philosophies and approaches that were possible. Probably the greatest influence on my educational thinking was my teacher Jerome Bruner. Bruner situated himself comfortably in the American progressive-pragmatist position and that has proved to be a comfortable stance for me as well.

The educational historian Ellen Lagemann has shrewdly pointed out that in the battles for the soul of American education, Edward Thorndike won, and John Dewey lost. On the Deweyian side are arrayed the majority of teachers and educationalists who associate themselves with progressive ideas—a focus on individual differences, constructivist learning, educational choices, a generous place for artistic activity and creativity, and so on. On the rival Thorndikean side are positioned the legion of politicians and policy makers who, for whatever reasons, favor traditional subjects, traditional teaching methods, and, above all, traditional methods of assessment—objective, short-answer, or multiple choice instruments. I think it is fair to say that nowadays, most parents and citizens in the United States also favor the traditional views; this stance would have been less true during earlier epochs of the 20th century.

I would speculate that some of the authorities in this volume are more sympathetic to traditional ideas, others tend toward progressive ideas, and still others struggle between the two sentiments. But it is clear to me that the three educationalists who have participated in this symposium are all sympathetic to progressive ideas—and so, for the most part, they have no quarrel with the uses to which MI ideas have been put.

Maxine Greene situates herself clearly in the progressive philosophical and educational camp of John Dewey; and indeed I consider Greene to be the embodiment of the Deweyian spirit that survives on the educational scene today. She gives two cheers for the approach and ideas that I have developed. But in her soft-spoken way, Greene expresses the wish that I had more frequently invoked the arts, the imagination, and human rights. I could take a defensive stand and cite places where I have touched on these issues. But I prefer to say that in a symposium on MI theory, such stretches would constitute a bridge too far.

Greene suggests that my emphasis may fall too much on the social science of psychology and not enough in the humanities. This may be more of a historical characterization than a contemporary point. As I see it, a century ago, the chief discipline that influenced education was philosophy (with Dewey at the forefront). Fifty years ago, the most influential discipline was psychology: The psychoanalyst Freud and the behaviorist Skinner soon came to be replaced by the cognitivists Piaget, Vygotsky, and Bruner. Nowadays, of course, it is the economists—until recently, those who are entranced by the marketplace—who increasingly call the tune in educational circles all around the world.

I almost said "economists and policy makers," but that would have been precisely the wrong thing to say at this juncture. Linda Darling-Hammond comes from the world of policy, but she is hardly entranced by market thinking. Indeed, when it comes to the social sciences, she is much more likely to invoke anthropology, sociology, or psychology than supply and demand, competition with China, or the need for tougher accountability rubrics. Her account of the uses—mostly constructive—to which MI theory has been put is so clear, comprehensive, and constructive, that I can only thank her and say, "Amen." I am pleased that President Barack Obama has had the benefit of her counsel.

In her charmingly arch manner, much acclaimed educator Deborah Meier reviews the ways in which she is sympathetic to MI theory and the ways in which she wishes that it would go further, or in a different direction. It is not surprising—and it is appropriate—that this venerable teacher and principal would have developed her own quite specific ideas about how institutions should be fashioned, how teachers should teach and coach, how students should learn. And, indeed, I'd be pleased to send my children or my grandchild to any school that Meier had designed and over which she presided.

I see our enterprises as complementary. As a social scientist, I develop concepts, definitions, and fledgling theories and put them forth for discussion: It is necessary to emphasize the distinctions that I consider to be important, while clearly delimiting my agenda and not attempting to cover all bases. I am not primarily concerned with the uses to which these ideas are put by practitioners, though of course I prefer that the applications are rigorous and benign.

As a practitioner (and also a popular writer), Meier is opportunistic; she eagerly draws upon ideas and concepts that advance her own agenda. At the same time, she is secure in her own progressive, democratic value system, vigilant that no misconceptions obtain and that no malignant pathways are pursued. And so she warns against any kind of overly strict classification system and also against the sins of IQ being visited as well on the fans of MI. The more time that I spend in schools, the more I can appreciate the points that she is emphasizing.

5. A PERSONAL REFLECTION

Ellen Winner's essay is characteristically modest, graceful, witty, and admirably laconic. Since I do not match her in these attributes, I can only thank her for them and thank her for her love and devotion over the years. Rest assured, the sentiments are fully reciprocated. I have learned a great deal—more than I can know or admit—from Ellen, and I trust that will remain true for many years to come.

FUTURE DIRECTIONS

While 25 years marks the right time to look backward, it may be appropriate, in closing, to cast my vision forward and to anticipate what work may be done in the spirit of MI in the coming decades. As I survey the landscape, I discern the following possibilities:

Additional Intelligences and Subintelligences

At present, I've recognized eight, possibly nine intelligences. Other possible intelligences have been nominated: Of all of them, I currently find "pedagogical/teaching intelligence" the most appealing. In striking contrast to other primates, all human beings have the potential to teach others;

and yet, even from an early age, we differ from one another in our capacities to teach effectively.

But I do not choose intelligences on the basis of their initial appeal. Rather, only those candidates that satisfy the eight criteria reasonably well should qualify. I've been very conservative over the years, adding only one intelligence in a quarter century! But I am happy to have other budding theorists apply the criteria. The major requirement is that one should not confound description with prescription. Intelligences are computational capacities that can be used in various ways, destructive as well as constructive. I discuss the uses of intelligences below.

Biological Research

As Michael Posner points out in his commentary, the biological evidence for MI theory—convincing at the time—seems anachronistic, in view of the tremendous progress over the past decades. Without question, the most important research to be done with reference to MI theory comes from neuroscience and genetics. Genetics research will reveal whether the different intelligences reflect different genetic patterns—or whether the genetics underlying various intellectual potentials and achievements are quite similar. Neuroscience will reveal the extent to which, and the ways in which, the various intellectual capacities are represented in the cortex and, as appropriate, in subcortical structures. Also, and to an extent that could not have been anticipated 25 years ago, the plasticity of representation of the various intelligences will be a topic of enduring interest. If, as Antonio Battro (2006) argues, half a brain is enough, then specific neural representations singled out in *Frames* represent options, but hardly obligatory sites.

Minds of the Future

My initial forays into education were designed around individual differences and multiple modes of presenting knowledge. I assumed the appropriateness of progressive educational goals, as realized in many schools, perhaps most brilliantly in the infant toddler centers and preschools of Reggio Emilia, in Italy. But, in a nod to traditional education, I focused much attention on the importance of mastering the disciplines and the necessity of disciplinary mastery before one undertakes the challenge of interdisciplinary work.

In more recent work, however, I have nominated five kinds of minds that, I believe, are crucial going forward (Gardner, 2007b). Some wags joked that I had dropped three of my intelligences; but in fact, I approach the "five minds" challenge as a policy maker, not as a psychologist or biologist.

Nor, surprisingly, many have asked about the relationship between the five minds and MI. Very briefly, the respectful mind depends heavily on interpersonal intelligence; the ethical mind requires both interpersonal intelligence and a certain degree of abstraction—hence logical intelligence.

Turning to the traditional cognitive minds, both the disciplinary mind and the creating mind can draw on any and all intelligences. Different disciplines evoke respective intelligences, and, of course, interdisciplinary work is likely to evoke multiple intelligences. Creative work draws on the same set of intelligences, but uses the intelligences to raise new questions, come up with new approaches, and arrive at unexpected responses. Creativity, as I (and some others) have come to see it, is more of an issue of personality and temperament than of intelligences per se.

Which leaves the fifth mind of the future—the synthesizing mind. In *Frames* I admitted that I had difficulty in explicating metaphor in terms of the multiple intelligences theory. An analogous difficulty surrounds the explanation of synthesizing—how we take in, evaluate, and then integrate vast amounts of information, in forms that make sense to ourselves and to others. I suspect that different synthesizers draw on different combinations of intelligences. In my own case, I suspect that the naturalist intelligence—classifying and reclassifying—plays a central role in my synthesizing activities.

Revealing my conservative side, I insist that one cannot think outside the box (creatively) unless one has a box—the job of the disciplined and the synthesizing minds. I find it useful, therefore, to cite Daniel Pink (2005) whose "whole new mind" includes storytelling, metaphor, and symphonic ways of thinking. Depending on the direction of events, these minds may be as important as or more important than the ones I specified.

Educational Applications, in and Outside Schools

Of course, by far the most numerous applications of MI theory have taken place in schools, in the United States and abroad. The new volume *Multiple Intelligences Around the World* (Chen et al., 2009) provides a singular opportunity to survey the many ways in which ingenious teachers, curators, librarians, and other professionals have made use of MI ideas, often without my knowledge, nearly always without my approval (though such approval is not necessary). I have every reason to expect that such experimentation will continue; and, as has happened in the past, I hope that those who have had positive experiences will find ways to share them with others.

Workplace and Life Applications

Even when one embraces a broad definition of education, the uses of MI theory are not restricted to that sphere. At the workplace, human resources teams are paying increasing attention to the intellectual profiles of their hires; and those in charge of assembling teams are also thinking in terms of which profiles of intelligence might be complementary or synergistic. The notion that different companies, or corporations, or spheres, might also exhibit distinctive profiles is also worth investigating. And such investigations may well turn up candidate intelligences that are worth considering seriously.

In this context, I should mention the best instantiation of MI theory that I have ever seen: the Explorama at Danfoss Universe in Denmark. In this theme park are arrayed a few dozen games or puzzles, each of which putatively calls upon a distinctive intelligence or set of intelligences. Anyone who spends half a day at the Explorama will rapidly pick up the idea of multiple intelligences, as well as the realization that he or she is not going to be equally successful at deploying each of the several intelligences. Moreover, thanks to a handheld personal assistant, individuals can predict their performance and evaluate the accuracy of their predictions, thus casting light on their intrapersonal intelligence. Especially appealing about the Explorama is that it can be enjoyed by individuals ranging in age from 5 to . . . you name it.

Computers, the Web, and Virtual Realities

Among the candidate intelligences that have been proposed, one of the most interesting is Digital Intelligence, put forth by Antonio Battro and Percy Denham (2007). What they call "the click option" could conceivably be a separate intelligence, though in my view, this capacity can readily be explained via logical and bodily intelligences.

Be that as it may, there is no question that the new digital media will be a boon for MI theory and vice versa. I could call for individualized education till the last year of the next millennium and it would make little difference; but the advent of increasingly powerful and versatile computers will make such advocacy unnecessary. In Web 2.0 and the virtual realities that it affords is ample space for the use of nearly all intelligences and combinations of intelligences. This potential will allow individuals and groups to learn and to share in ways that could not have been imagined even a few decades ago. These advances can, of course, take place without explicit mention of MI theory—and yet its judicious use could benefit theorists, educators, and ordinary users.

Intelligences for What?

For the better part of my scholarly life, I've studied capacities like intelligence, creativity, and leadership in an amoral way. Not immoral, surely, but without regard to how these capacities are being used, and this tack seems appropriate. Both Nelson Mandela and Slobodan Milosevic have considerable interpersonal intelligence: It is the uses to which that intelligence is put that distinguishes them. A study of leadership could focus on only admired leaders; but then it would fail to elicit lessons contained in the biographies of such individuals as Genghis Khan, Adolf Hitler, and Josep Stalin.

Nonetheless, as a citizen and human being, I care mightily about the ways in which our abilities are deployed. The problem in the American prosecution of the Vietnam War was not the absence of "the best and the brightest;" rather it was the use to which their intellects and their educations were put. The same can be said for the architects of the Iraqi war or of the financial instruments that led to the worldwide fiscal meltdown of late 2008.

Accordingly, with my close colleagues Mihaly Csikszentmihalyi, William Damon, and many other researchers, I've been studying the uses to which intelligences, leadership, and creativity have been put. In the Good-Work project, and more recently in the GoodPlay project, we have been trying to understand how it is that certain individuals use their faculties in a responsible, ethical way; why too many individuals do not; and what can be done in the future to enhance the number of good persons, good citizens, good workers, and good players. No one could have predicted that MI theory would end up at this place; but it is a good place for me to be, and I expect to be working on good work for the indefinite future (Fischman et al., 2004; Gardner, 2007a; Gardner, Csikszentmihalyi, & Damon, 2001).

CLOSING THOUGHTS

In closing, I want to reiterate my appreciation to Branton Shearer, who conceived and collated these contributions; and I want to add my thanks to the 10 scholars and colleagues who took time to record their thoughts about MI theory. I have learned from each of you; I hope that you have also learned from one another's reactions and from my responses. Finally, and most ardently, I hope that you, the reader, will join in the conversation. Whether my ideas are ultimately accepted wholly, in part, or not at all, I am certain that the discussions thereof have borne fruit—and I suspect that they will continue to do so.

REFERENCES

Battro, A. (2006). *Half a mind is enough*. New York: Cambridge University Press.
Battro, A., & Denham, P. (2007). *La educacion digital*. Buenos Aires: Pan American Books.

Chen, J., Moran, S., & Gardner, H. (2009). *Multiple intelligences around the world.* San Francisco: Jossey Bass.

Fischman, W., Solomon, B., Greenspan, D., & Gardner, H. (2004). *Making good: How young people cope with moral dilemmas at work.* Cambridge, MA: Harvard University Press.

Gardner, H. (1983). *Frames of mind: The theory of multiple intelligences.* New York: Basic Books.

Gardner, H. (1991). *The unschooled mind.* New York: Basic Books

Gardner, H. (1993a). *Multiple intelligences: The theory in practice.* New York: Basic Books.

Gardner, H. (1993b). *Creating minds.* New York: Basic Books.

Gardner, H., with Emma Laskin (1995). *Leading minds.* New York: Basic Books.

Gardner, H. (1997). *Extraordinary minds.* New York: Basic Books.

Gardner, H. (1999a). *Intelligence reframed.* New York: Basic Books.

Gardner, H. (1999b). *The disciplined mind.* New York: Simon and Schuster.

Gardner, H. (2006a). *Multiple intelligences: The theory in practice.* New York: Basic Books.

Gardner, H. (2006b). On failing to grasp the core of multiple intelligences theory: A response to Visser et al. *Intelligence, 34*(5), 503–505.

Gardner, H. (Ed). (2007a). *Responsibility at work.* San Francisco: Jossey Bass.

Gardner, H. (2007b). *Five minds for the future.* Boston: Harvard Business School Press.

Gardner, H. (2008). "Multiple intelligences in the twenty-first century." In G. Mazur (Ed.), *Thirty year commemoration to the life of A. E. Luria.* New York: Semenko Foundation.

Gardner, H., Csikszentmihalyi, M., & Damon, W. (2001). *Good work: When excellence and ethics meet.* New York: Basic Books.

Gardner, H., & Moran, S. (2006). The science in multiple intelligences theory: A response to Lynn Waterhouse. *Educational Psychologist, 41*(4), 227–232.

Herrnstein, R., & Murray, C. (1994). *The bell curve.* New York: Free Press.

Pink, D. (2005). *A whole new mind.* New York: Riverhead Books.

Schaler, J. (Ed.) (2006). *Howard Gardner under fire.* LaSalle, IL: Open Court.

About the Editor and the Contributors

C. Branton Shearer is a neuropsychologist who has taught about the creative and practical applications of multiple intelligences since 1990 at Kent State University in Kent, Ohio. He is the creator of the Multiple Intelligences Developmental Scales (MIDAS, www.MIResearch.org), which have been translated into 12 languages and implemented by educators and researchers in more than 20 different countries. He is the founder of the American Educational Research Association Special Interest Group Multiple Intelligences: Theory and Practice. His books include *Creating Extra-Ordinary Teachers*, coauthored with Mike Fleetham and published in 2008, and *MIndful Education for ADHD Students: Differentiating Curriculum and Instruction Using Multiple Intelligences*, coauthored with Victoria Proulx-Schirduan and Karen I. Case and published in 2009. He has also written *The MIDAS: Professional Manual* (1996, 2007), along with six additional books guiding the practical applications of the MIDAS assessment to enhance teaching, education, and career planning.

Avram Noam Chomsky (Hebrew: ψθσμωφ ![ων !ρβα) (born December 7, 1928) is an American linguist, philosopher, political activist, author, and lecturer. He is an Institute Professor and professor emeritus of linguistics at the Massachusetts Institute of Technology. Chomsky is credited with the creation of the theory of generative grammar, considered to be one of the

Photo of Norm Chomsky by Duncan Rawlinson / www.thelastminuteblog.com. Photo of Marc Hauser by Lilan Hauser. Photo Mihaly Csikszentmihalyi by Chris Csikszentmihalyi. Photo of Ellen Winner by Benjamin Gardner. Photo of Howard Gardner by Rodrigo Sepúlveda, *El Tiempo Newspaper*.

most significant contributions to the field of linguistics made in the 20th century. He also helped spark the cognitive revolution in psychology through his review of B. F. Skinner's Verbal Behavior, in which he challenged the behaviorist approach to the study of behavior and language dominant in the 1950s. His naturalistic approach to the study of language has affected the philosophy of language and mind. He is also credited with the establishment of the Chomsky hierarchy, a classification of formal languages in terms of their generative power. He has lectured at many universities here and abroad, and is the recipient of numerous honorary degrees and awards. He has written and lectured widely on linguistics, philosophy, intellectual history, contemporary issues, international affairs and U.S. foreign policy. His most recent books are *A New Generation Draws the Line*; *New Horizons in the Study of Language and Mind*; *Rogue States*; *9-11*; *Understanding Power*; *On Nature and Language*; *Pirates and Emperors, Old and New*; *Chomsky on Democracy and Education*; *Middle East Illusions*; *Hegemony or Survival*; *Imperial Ambitions*; *Failed States*; *Perilous Power*; *Interventions*; *Inside Lebanon*; *What We Say Goes: Conversations on U.S. Power in a Changing World*; and *The Essential Chomsky*.

Marc Hauser is Harvard College professor of psychology, organismic and evolutionary biology, and biological anthropology. He is an adjunct professor at the Harvard Graduate School of Education and codirector of the Program in Neurosciences, Mind, Brain and Behavior; a fellow at the Center for Ethics; and director of the Cognitive Evolution Lab. Hauser's research focuses on the evolutionary and developmental foundations of the human mind, with the specific goal of understanding which mental capacities are shared with other nonhuman primates and which are uniquely human. Central questions include the following: What are the evolutionarily ancient building blocks of our capacity for language, mathematics, music, and morality? What were the selective pressures that led to a change in mental representation from the divergence point with the last common primate ancestor? To what extent is the architecture of the mind composed of domain-specific reasoning mechanisms? How do such mechanisms channel the organism's experiences in the world, allowing it to acquire a mature state of knowledge? His publications include technical papers in biology, psychology, neuroscience, anthropological, developmental, and evolution journals, as well as trade books and articles, including most recently *Moral Minds*.

Michael I. Posner is currently professor emeritus at the University of Oregon and adjunct professor of psychology in psychiatry at the Weill Medical College of Cornell, where he served as founding director of the Sackler Institute. Posner is best known for his work with Marcus Raichle on imaging the human brain during cognitive tasks. He has worked on the anatomy, circuitry, development, and genetics of three attentional networks underlying alertness, orienting, and voluntary control of thoughts and ideas. His methods for measuring these networks have been applied to neurological, psychiatric, and developmental disorders. His current research involves training of attention in young children to understand the interaction of specific experience and genes in shaping attention. With Mary K. Rothbart, he has written a new volume, *Educating the Human Brain*, relating his work to education.

Mihaly Csikszentmihalyi, one of the world's leading authorities on the psychology of creativity, is the Distinguished Professor of Psychology at the School of Behavioral and Organizational Sciences at Claremont Graduate University and codirector of the Quality of Life Research Center. He is also emeritus professor of human development at the University of Chicago, where he chaired the Department of Psychology. His life's work has been to study what makes people truly happy. Drawing upon years of systematic research, he developed the concept of "flow" as a description of the rare mental state associated with feelings of optimal satisfaction and fulfillment. His analysis of the internal and external conditions giving rise to flow show that it is almost always linked to circumstances of high challenge when personal skills are used to the utmost. He is the author of the hugely influential *Flow: The Psychology of Optimal Experience* (1990) and thirteen other books, translated into 25 languages, and some 228 research articles. His latest books are *Experience Sampling Method: Measuring the Quality of Everyday Life* (2007) and *A Life Worth Living: Contributions to Positive Psychology* (2006).

Charles Murray, the W. H. Brady Scholar at the American Enterprise Institute, is best known for his books *Losing Ground: American Social Policy, 1950–1980* (1984) and, with Richard J. Herrnstein, *The Bell Curve: Intelligence and Class Structure in American Life* (1994). His most recent book is *Real Education: Four Simple Truths for Bringing America's Schools Back to Reality* (2008). His career prior to joining AEI in 1990 includes 6 years of work in rural Thailand and a decade evaluating federal social programs as a research scientist at the American Institutes for Research. Murray obtained a BA in history from Harvard in 1965 and a PhD in political science from the Massachusetts Institute of Technology in 1974.

James Robert Flynn is professor emeritus at the University of Otago in Dunedin, New Zealand. He is known for his documentation of the Flynn effect, that is, the rise of IQ scores from one generation to another in all parts of the world. Flynn is the author of seven books, including *What Is Intelligence?* (2007), described by Robert J. Sternberg as a masterful work that will influence thinking about intelligence for many years to come. His research interests include measuring critical acumen, the current U.S. political and intellectual scene (*Where Have All the Liberals Gone?* [2008]), the justification of humane ideals (*How to Defend Humane Ideals* [2000]), illumination of the classics of political philosophy, and race, class, and IQ. He currently sits on the editorial board of *Intelligence* and was named Distinguished Contributor of the Year by the International Society of Intelligence Research. Originally from Washington DC, Flynn arrived in New Zealand in 1963.

He is currently a Visiting Fellow at the Russell Sage Foundation in New York.

Linda Darling-Hammond is the Charles E. Ducommun Professor of Education at Stanford University, where she has launched the Stanford Educational Leadership Institute and the School Redesign Network. She is a former president of the American Educational Research Association and member of the National Academy of Education. Among her more than 300 publications are *Preparing Teachers for a Changing World: What Teachers Should Learn and Be Able to Do* (with John Bransford, for the National Academy of Education), winner of the Pomeroy Award from AACTE; *Teaching as the Learning Profession: A Handbook of Policy and Practice* (coedited with Gary Sykes), which received the National Staff Development Council's Outstanding Book Award for 2000; and *The Right to Learn: A Blueprint for Schools That Work*, recipient of the American Educational Research Association's Outstanding Book Award for 1998.

Maxine Greene has been at the forefront of educational philosophy for well more than a half century as a teacher, lecturer, and author. She is the founder and director of the Maxine Greene Foundation for the Arts and Social Imagination, which has given grants to young artists whose work has a social edge and that sponsors a bimonthly dialogical "salon" focusing on contemporary literature. She still teaches at Teachers College as professor of philosophy and education (emerita) and at the Lincoln Center Institute for the Arts in Education. She is a former editor of the Teachers College Record and a past president of the Philosophy of Education Society and the American Educational Research Association. As philosopher in residence in the Lincoln Center Institute for the Arts in Education, she has become much engaged with the study of imagination and, in addition, the participatory approach to works of art. She hopes she has made a contribution to a recognition of the importance of "wide-awakeness" in classrooms and in encounters with the forms of art. Alfred Schutz has described this as "the highest plane of consciousness"; Paulo Freire, as "conscientization";

John Dewey, as breaking through "the crust of consciousness" and somehow replacing the "anaesthetic" with aesthetic experiences. At a time when so many public school students are bored or afflicted by a sense of the irrelevance or futility of their schooling, she argues for encouragement of imagination and connections of subject matter with contemporary issues.

Deborah W. Meier is often considered the founder of the modern small-schools movement. She has spent more than 40 years working in our urban public K–12 schools—as parent, teacher, and principal. She has written and spoken about her work, starting as a kindergarten teacher. Her publications include two books describing the small public schools she founded in New York's East Harlem and Boston's Roxbury neighborhood, *The Power of Their Ideas*, and *In Schools We Trust*. She was a founding member of the Coalition of Essential Schools with Ted Sizer and an initiator of the National Board for Professional Teaching Standards and winner of a MacArthur Fellowship for her work as an educator. She has continued her interest in young children and leads a new effort to build on the strengths of childhood, at indefenseofchildhood.org. Many call her the mother of the modern small-school movement. She is currently affiliated with New York University's Steinhardt School of Education.

Ellen Winner is professor of psychology at Boston College and senior research associate at Project Zero, Harvard Graduate School of Education. She received her PhD from Harvard University in 1978. Her research focuses on learning and cognition in the arts. She is the author of more than 100 articles and four books: *Invented Worlds: The Psychology of the Arts* (1982); *The Point of Words: Children's Understanding of Metaphor and Irony* (1988); *Gifted Children: Myths and Realities* (1997), translated into six languages and winner of the Alpha Sigma Nu National Jesuit Book Award in Science; and *Studio Thinking: The Real Benefits of Visual Arts Education* (2007), coauthored with Lois Hetland, Shirley Veenema, and Kimberly Sheridan. She received the Rudolf Arnheim Award for Outstanding Research by a Senior

Scholar in Psychology and the Arts from the American Psychological Association.

Howard E. Gardner is the John H. and Elisabeth A. Hobbs Professor of Cognition and Education at the Harvard Graduate School of Education. Among numerous honors, Gardner received a MacArthur Fellowship in 1981. In 1990, he was the first American to receive the University of Louisville's Grawemeyer Award in Education and in 2000 he received a fellowship from the John S. Guggenheim Memorial Foundation. He has received honorary degrees from 22 colleges and universities, including institutions in Chile, Ireland, Israel, and Italy. In 2004 he was named an Honorary Professor at East China Normal University in Shanghai. In 2005 he was selected by *Foreign Policy* and *Prospect* magazines as one of 100 most influential public intellectuals in the world.

The author of more than 20 books, translated into 27 languages, and several hundred articles, Gardner is best known in educational circles for his theory of multiple intelligences, a critique of the notion that there exists but a single human intelligence that can be assessed by standard psychometric instruments. Building on his studies of intelligence, Gardner has also authored *Leading Minds*, *Changing Minds*, and *Extraordinary Minds*. Other recent books by Gardner include *The Disciplined Mind*, *The Development and Education of the Mind*, and *Multiple Intelligences: New Horizons*. *Gardner Under Fire* (2006) contains a set of critiques to which Gardner has responded, as well as an autobiography. Gardner's newest book, *Five Minds for the Future*, was published in 2007.

Index